JUDGES
and
RUTH

STEPHEN DRAY

Christian Focus

To my mother
Edna Dray

and to my parents in law
Peter and Agnes Tucker

© Stephen Dray
ISBN 1 85792 323 5
Published in 1997 by
Christian Focus Publications
Geanies House, Fearn, Ross-shire
IV20 1TW, Great Britain

Contents

JUDGES

RUTH

Introduction

The Old Testament narrative books tend to finish rather like a good televised serial story! Just at the point when you and I are anxious to know what will happen next, the book comes to an end! Take Genesis for example. The latter part of the book is woven around the promises made to Abraham and his family. Little by little we see God working out his purposes (often in highly unpromising circumstances) until, in chapter 50, we are brought to the point where we are asking, 'How then is God going to fulfil his plans?' This question is re-enforced by the description of Joseph's death-bed affirmation: 'God will surely come to your aid and take you up out of this land to the land he promised on oath to Abraham, Isaac and Jacob' (Genesis 50:24). But we are left 'suspended in mid air'. It is not until we turn over the page and begin to read Exodus that the answer begins to unfold!

The Book of Joshua is little different. The account of the initial conquest is given up to the death of Joshua himself. Again we are left anticipating the sequel. Once again our anticipation is heightened by Joshua's final address (recorded in Joshua 24). There Joshua reminds the people of their past experience of God's blessing; he reminds them of their election (*verses 2-4*), redemption (*verses 5-7*) and their recent experience of the Lord's actions on their behalf (*verses 11-13*). The people recognise the truth of what Joshua said (*verses 16-18*) and pledge themselves to the Lord (see, especially, *verse 21*, 'we will serve the LORD') and his Law (*verses 25f.*). What can God not do with a people thus devoted to him?

There remained, of course, much to be done. A

5

comparison between Joshua and the early chapters of Judges indicates that, though a general conquest had been undertaken, pockets of resistance remained. The war had been won, the decisive battles had apparently occurred. Effort might be required to secure peace but it now seemed achievable.

So, the people's pledge and their past experience of God promised well for the future: despite Joshua's warning (*verses 19f.*). And on this optimistic note of expected victory the Book of Joshua closes. Jensen says:

> Thus they [had] entered into the promised blessings of the inheritance – victory, prosperity and happiness – which is the life God would always have His people lead. They were surrounded by enemies; indeed some enemies still lived within their boundaries. But if they would obey God and His commands concerning these enemies, they would have the power of the Almighty with them.[1]

Moreover, as Keddie notes, the 'momentum' was not with their enemies but with them: the Canaanites were terrified of the Israelites.[2]

So we turn over the page and, with high hopes, begin to read the sequel.

---

1. Jensen, Irving, *Survey of the Old Testament*, Moody Press, p.154.
2. Keddie, Gordon, page 9.

Useful Background Information

A Time - Line

Establishing absolute dates for Biblical events prior to the time of David is difficult and largely depends upon two issues. The first relates to whether or not 1 Kings 6:1 refers to actual calendar years or 12 generations (perhaps 300 years?). The second area of debate is how best to harmonise the discoveries of archaeological research to the biblical story.

Most students conclude that a period of 300 years 'fits' better than one of nearly 500 years for the time from the Exodus to the dedication of Solomon's temple. However, the longer span is not impossible and does seem to be the 'plain' meaning of the text in 1 Kings 6:1. It has been assumed in this commentary.

A further complication is that there does seem to have been some 'overlap' between some of the judges, so dates for the period are bound to be uncertain.

The following chart might, however, offer approximate dates for the period from Abraham to David. It is based on work by J.H. Walton (*Chronological Charts of the Old Testament*, Grand Rapids, Zondervan, 1979).

2166	Birth of Abraham
1876	Jacob and his family move to Egypt
1446	The Exodus
1385-1377	Oppression by Cushan-rishathaim (Judges 3:8)
1377-1337	Othniel (Judges 3:9-11)
1337-1319	Oppression by Eglon (Judges 3:12-14)

1319-1239	Ehud (Judges 3:15-30)
1260-1260	Shamgar (Judges 3:31)
1259-1239	Oppression by Jabin (Judges 4:2-3)
1239-1199	Deborah (Judges 4:4 - 5:31)
1199-1192	Midianite oppression (Judges 6:1-6. Does the Book of Ruth fit in here?)
1152-1149	Civil War: Abimelech (Judges 9)
1149-1126	Tola (Judges 10:1,2)
1126-1104	Jair (Judges 10:3-6)
1104-1086	Ammonite oppression (Judges 10:7-9)
1086-1080	Jephthah (Judges 10:10 - 12:7)
1080-1072	Ibzan (Judges 12:8-10)
1072-1062	Elon (Judges 12:11-12)
1062-1055	Abdon (Judges 12:13-15)
1115-1075	Philistine oppression (Judges 13:1)
1075-1055	Samson (Judges 13:2 - 16:31)
1051-1011	Saul
1011-971	David
971-931	Solomon

The Geography of Palestine

The map shows the main peoples and locations mentioned in the Books of Joshua and Judges. Of particular importance for understanding the book are a recognition that a spine of mountains and hills stretches the length of the land except for the Valley of Jezreel which opens up from the Mediterannean Sea near Carmel and extends across to Galilee and the Jordan Valley.

This was often the route which enemies took to attack Israel (as it was at the time of Gideon). At the time of the Judges the Phoenician 'Sea Peoples' (known in the Bible as the Philistines) were settling along the coast and

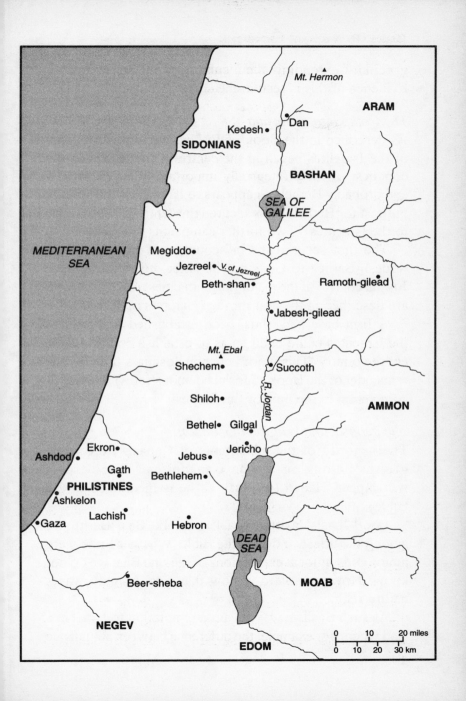

gradually extending their sphere of influence inland. Evidence of this is seen in the story of Samson.

The Campaign of Joshua

As described in the Book of Joshua, the initial campaign of the Israelites began in the centre of the land with the conquest of the strategically important cities of Jericho and probably Bethel (Ai appears to have been the military outpost for Bethel). This secured the centre of the country to the Israelites. Two further campaigns followed.

The first secured the hill-country to the south from Kadesh-Barnea to Gibeon. The latter, northwards, gave Joshua control of the major northern cities. All these events are described in the first thirteen chapters of Joshua.

A firm base had, thus, been established upon which the Israelites could build so as to establish control of the entire country. This work began in Joshua's time (as the remainder of the Book of Joshua demonstrates). It awaited completion in the time of the Judges.

The peoples and religion of Canaan

The majority of the inhabitants of Canaan were tribal groups belonging to the Canaanites. These tribes worshipped Hadad (or Baal, as he is mentioned in the Bible).

Local 'baals' existed: Baal Peor and Baal Berith are among the titles we find in the Bible. Whether these were junior gods or local expressions of the one Baal we do not know. However, we do know that Baal religion was a nature religion.

As such Baalism was always a temptation to Israel in a land where, for example, the difference between abundance and famine could depend on the uncertainties of the weather. The manipulative magical practices of Baalism designed to guarantee what was needed seemed to offer certainty where simple faith in the LORD might appear to default! Doubtless this was rationalised. It was not that the LORD was being abandoned but rather a necessary supplement was being added. The Book of Judges is designed to 'give the lie' to such a view.

The Judges

Leadership in ancient Israel was relatively unstructured. However, certain people rose to a place of leadership because of their natural and spiritual giftings. While they did not come to hold an official 'office', their leadership was recognised and their lead followed. This is true of the 'Judges'; men and women who were recognised to have been gifted and appointed by God for leadership of the people.

The judges had no official religious functions (that responsibility lay with the priests and Levites) and they were not regarded as being the spokespersons of God (in the way a prophet was; though Samuel is something of an exception since he combined both the role of Judge and Prophet in his own ministry).

Rather Judges were people with practical skills and wisdom which enabled them to offer the people a lead in war and in peace.

References to other commentaries

Judges has not, until recently, been well served by the commentators. The Tyndale Old Testament Commentary (IVP, 1968) volume by Arthur E. Cundall is rapidly dat-

11

ing and preoccupied with historical background; several, e.g. A. Lewis (Everyman Bible Commentary, Moody Press, 1979), P. P. Enns (Bible Study Commentary, Zondervan, 1982), C. J. Goslinga (Bible Students Commentary, Zondervan, 1986) offer a detailed explanation but provide little theological insight or practical application; Graeme Auld (Joshua, Judges and Ruth, St. Andrew Press, 1984) is so destructive as to be of little value and J. A. Soggin (SCM, 1981) is only marginally better though offering some theological insights. Gordon J. Keddie (Welwyn Bible Commentary, Evangelical Press, 1985) is conservative exposition and application but as with so much evangelical work on narrative books suffers from a tendency to over-indulge in typology and virtually ignores chapters 17-21.

However, Michael Wilcock (The Bible Speaks Today, IVP, 1992) is very good and Dale R. Davis, *Such a Great Salvation* (Baker, 1990) is excellent. Both supply first class explanation and application. James B. Jordan (Trinity Biblical Commentary, Geneva Ministries, 1985) is bizarre in places but the discerning reader will use it with some profit.

Several recent studies have been published on the book. Among the most interesting is Lilian R Klein, *The Triumph of Irony in the Book of Judges* (Sheffield Academic Press, 1989).

1:1-2:5: Trust and Obey

Initially all went well for the Israelites. The people sought the Lord's direction and help (*verses 1, 2*) in the manner he had appointed (compare Numbers 27:18-21). Following the specific advice that he gave them that **Judah is to go**, they quickly experience the fulfilment of God's promise: **I have given the land into their hands**. God went with them and brought them victory (see, especially, *verse 19a*). Successes followed for both Judah/Simeon (*verses 3-26*) and also for the other tribes (*verses 27ff.*).

Obediently, Judah responded to the word of God and remarkable successes followed! The author of Judges records that **they struck down ten thousand men at Bezek** (*verse 4*); an unimaginably vast victory for the relatively unpopulated world of the time. Moreover, the king of Bezek was no local clan-chief but a mighty emperor with many people groups subject to him (*verse 7*).

Success followed success. Jerusalem itself was captured (*verse 8*) and, significantly, victory was experienced wherever Judah went, whether in the **hill country** or the south country (or **Negev**) or in the low-lying **western foothills** (*verse 9*). But victory in different terrain and over a wide geographical area was not all that was experienced. Mighty cities fell to the Judahites. **Hebron**, one of the great towns of Palestine was taken (*verse 10*). Significantly, we are reminded of its other name: **Kiriath Arba**. Arba was the name of the father of the Anakim (compare, Joshua 14:15 and 15:13), the giants before whom the Israelites had trembled in the wilderness. Apparently this city was their stronghold but it was taken so summarily that it gets but half a verse! In addition, the great cultural city of the region, **Kiriath Sepher**, the city of books, was subdued (*verses 11ff.*). To destroy the military and cultural centres was to destroy the civilisation built around them. Victory for the Judahites was total!

At this point, and perhaps surprisingly, we are introduced to a bit of family history (*verses 11-15*). However, when the Scriptures offer us little (or big) surprises we should not pass over them too rapidly. We need to ask the question why such incidents were recorded. Some commentators suggest that we are intended to see this story about **Othniel** and **Acsah** as something of a parable and develop this idea in two possible directions. Here we are introduced to two young people who were ready to venture in faithful obedience to God and found him fully able to supply their needs. Not only the nation but the individual could expect God's help when they lived in humble dependence on him. Or, perhaps, we are intended to see in them a mirror image of what God was looking for in the people as a whole. If this is so, disappointment quickly follows for, increasingly, the story takes a less than happy turn.

Initially we are offered further accounts of victory (*verses 17, 18*); although we might 'smell a rat' in verse 18 when we are told that **Judah also took Gaza, Ashkelon and Ekron**, since elsewhere in the Old Testament we are told that there were *five*, not three, cities of the Philistines! Was the Judahite success beginning to run out of steam?

This certainly appears to be the case in the descriptions which are subsequently recounted – Judah failed to gain a hold on the lowlands, where the chariots of the Canaanites gave them the upper hand (*verse 19*). Anyone with a basic knowledge of Palestine will immediately realise the significance of this. James Jordan notes that:

The plains were in the center [sic] of the land of promise. The continuing strength of the Canaanites had effectively divided Judah and Simeon from the rest of the tribes. Over the centuries, this isolation brought about cultural division, and caused more and more trouble until the two kingdoms split from one another. Thus do minor compromises grow into major troubles.[3]

A brief but significant flashback is then recorded; faithful and elderly **Caleb** had led the rout of **Hebron** (*verse 20*, compare *verse 10*) and it was given to him as God had promised through his servant Moses. By way of (surely intended) contrast we are told that **Benjamin** failed to secure **Jerusalem** (*verse 21*).

From this point onwards the story rapidly plunges downhill into darkness. The success of **Joseph** (*verses 22-26*) stands out like a beacon amid the accounts of **Manasseh**'s failure to exterminate the inhabitants of **Beth Shan** etc. (*verse 27*) and the record that the Canaanites were not exterminated but dwelt in the land as subjects (*verses 29-30*). More serious was the fact that in some places the situation was reversed: **Asher** failed so miserably that the Canaanites held the upper hand. They 'lived among the Canaanite inhabitants'. But worst of all was the situation of **Dan**. They failed to dislodge the Canaanites and had to seek 'alternative accommodation' (*verse 34* and compare 18:1ff.).

---

3. Jordan, James, page 14.

Thus, a careful study of a map reveals that the Israelites were only able to hold the hill country rather like modern guerillas. They had failed entirely to establish themselves as God had promised. Indeed, as verse 35 indicates, the places where Joshua had been buried (**Mount Heres**, compare *2:9*) and where he had experienced his most spectacular victory (**Aijalon**, see Joshua 10:12) were now in Amorite hands, behind a sort of established frontier (*verse 36*).

But why this 'day of small things'? Chapter 1 offers a hint (*verse 19*). The military capability of the plains-people was too great for the limited resources of the Israelites. They could only get the upper hand where the chariots were valueless.

Yet can the writer of Judges expect us to take this comment seriously? Surely the entire story of the Israelites up to this point has been of God's intervention to turn their impossibilities into his victories. Their God – who had subdued Pharaoh, divided the Red Sea and the Jordan, fed millions of his people in a barren wilderness for forty years and had brought the walls of Jericho tumbling down – was surely not going to be baulked in his purposes by a few Canaanite chariots! Doubtless, then, we are intended to ask the question, 'Whatever the human reasons for failure, why does God not appear to be working among his people now?'

We are not left long to discover the answer! Moreover, when it comes it is God himself who speaks in the person of the **angel of the Lord** (*2:1*). This mysterious angel appears frequently in the Old Testament from Genesis 16 onwards. When he appears he is distinguished from other angels and when he speaks he not merely speaks God's words but is recognised as God himself. Some, therefore, identify the Angel with the Son of God. Whether or not this is true, the Angel had been sent before Israel to ensure their success (Exodus 23:20-23) and appears as captain of the LORD's host in Joshua 5:13ff..

Bokim may possibly be another name for Bethel. Whether or not this is so, the Israelites seemed to have gathered for a national convocation, possibly some form of war-council.

While they were there the Angel arrived from **Gilgal**. This is immensely significant. When the people entered the land they had pledged themselves to the Lord there and he had guaranteed their success (Joshua 5:13). Perhaps the people were complaining that he had failed them. In reality the Angel revealed that the boot was on the other foot: the people had failed their part of the 'bargain' and this in two ways. They had been told that their blessing depended on their obedience (Deuteronomy 30:16) and, in particular, that they were to make no covenant with the Canaanites and no compromise with their religion (Exodus 23:32f; 34:10-16). It was their unfaithfulness that had brought disaster. Later (chapters 4, 5), the Lord would prove that the chariots of the Canaanites were no problem to him! Equally, later chapters demonstrate that these two faults characterised the life of the people throughout the period of the Judges – in an ever more serious way.

Confronted with their sin the people **wept** and **offered sacrifices** (*verse 5*). We may, however, question their sincerity since there is no evidence of respite. Tears can sometimes be the result of having been caught out – not genuine sorrow. The Lord looks for rent hearts not garments (Psalm 51:17; Joel 2:12-14). Thus, as Lewis points out, 'true repentance must go beyond tears of sorrow and achieve a right-about-face, a turning of one's entire self from sin to a walk that pleases God'.[4]

But what has all this got to do with us? We need to see that we, too, are the people of God. We, too, are called to avoid all compromise with enemies whether within or without. There can be no compromise with the world nor any acceptance of sin. Although the enemies we are facing are mighty (and the New Testament never underestimates the power of the opposition, see Ephesians 6:12), they are no excuse for our failure. The only excuse a powerless church and a defeated Christian has is its, or his or her, disobedience. Defeat is not part of God's programme for us, ineffectiveness is not his plan. The 'day of small things' is a ground only for self-examination and penitence. Yet we can always hide behind apparently good excuses and, tacitly at least, blame God. We always have enemies with chariots! But God's programme for his church and his people is growth and, like the ancient Israelites, we have our past experience to strengthen our confidence and resolve.

Moreover, we need to learn to trust God. One cannot help feeling that, by and large, the people won the victories which they were able to achieve with their own resources. It was when they were at the end of themselves that they failed to look to God. How easily we can do the same. Our vision for the Lord's work is often no greater than our own strength.

---

4. Lewis, page 26.

Perhaps, then, the Saviour (prefigured in the Angel?) is calling us away from our compromise and small ambitions to loving obedience and victory. May his work in our hearts be deeper than that recorded in 2:5!

There is one final word, so typical of this book. Amid the judgement is a word of grace (*verse 3*). The people are not totally cut off as was to be expected. God left time for penitence. May we too redeem it.

Questions:

1. It is easy for us to read this passage and point the finger at our nation. However, the people of Israel were first and foremost the 'congregation of the LORD'. What might we learn as believers and church-members from our failures in the light of this passage?

2. Reflect on the example of Othniel and Acsah (1:11-15). What lessons might you and I learn from them?

3. What do you think are the characteristic marks of true repentance?

2:6-3:6: The downward spiral of disobedience and defeat

It is a feature of Hebrew writing that often a story, or part of it, is told twice over with slight differences of emphasis in order to derive different lessons from the same events. This is true here. The same period of Israel's history as occupied 1:1-2:5 is reintroduced, but the lessons to be learnt are different.

As we look at these verses it is clear that they were intended to teach the danger of resting upon the experience of past generations (*2:6-15*). Verses 6-9 repeat Joshua 24:28-31 but with one significant difference: in Judges the Lord's dealings with the Israelites are said to have been **great** (*verse 7*). Joshua and the elders had seen much success as they rested in the Lord. But it is easy for the next generation under such circumstances to presume upon such blessing (and even the generation who have received the blessing not to pass on the knowledge of it in an adequate way). Then when things start to go wrong the new generation shows that it has not the faith of that which has gone before it. Doubtless the generation after Joshua were aware of the nation's past history; but they **knew neither the LORD nor what he had done for Israel** (*verse 10*). In other words their knowledge was not something that had become personal and led to a loving obedience and trust in the Lord (this is what knowledge of God usually means in the Bible). Rather, various faithless attempts were adopted to 'bolster up' the situation. Any respite in such circumstances is, however, only temporary and any apparent blessing illusory. Powerlessness results and leads

to successive defeats. This is what is described in this paragraph. The new generation did not have that intimate
knowledge of the Lord which had characterised Joshua
the **servant of the Lord** (*verse 8*) and his colleagues. As a
result they had not seen the mighty deeds of God themselves and they were insufficiently aware of their past history, even second hand, to be able to derive any benefit
from it (*verse 10b*). The result was that they turned to the
religions of the land they had begun to conquer. We know
that they never, in their own minds, exchanged one religion for another. Rather they looked for help from the
gods of the land in matters in which the Lord seemed unable to help them. But the writer of Judges knew better:
They **did evil ... [and] forsook the LORD** (*verses 11,12*).
Rather than turn to self-examination they turned to self-
help. But such flabby religion led to flabby people, without the will to resist the Lord's enemies (*verse 14*). The
final result was utter defeat (*verse 15*). Yet, sadly, the people failed to realise their true situation: it was the Lord
into whose hands they had fallen (*verses 14f.*).

This a lesson we need to learn. The twentieth-century
church in Britain has reproduced this picture almost
exactly. In the early years the churches were able to rest
upon the success and the momentum of the past. But
gradually, as the tide turned against it more and more,
there was little evidence of penitence: only numerous
attempts to shore up shaky structures. Spirituality, even
among the faithful, went into rapid decline. Hope was lost
and 'great distress' became and to some extent remains
the situation today. The choice is ours: will we return to
the Lord of our fathers or continue to grieve the Lord and

experience his wrath (*verses 13-14*) by our efforts at faithless self-help?

A further lesson here is the danger of looking to the Lord for what Arthur Cundall calls 'crash-aid' (*verses 16-23*).[5] These verses summarise the remainder of the main section of the Book of Judges (3:7-16:31), a period of 200-400 years.[6] As such, they issue a very important warning. Even in their **great distress** (*verse 15*), the people refused to turn back to the Lord. This was despite the fact that the Lord encouraged their return by granting them leaders who were able to bring them success again (*verses 16, 18*). Even in such circumstances **they would not listen to their judges** (*verse 17*). Even where there was evidence of repentance the sequel indicated that their penitence was, at best, partial. All too quickly (**unlike their fathers, they quickly turned from the way**, *verse 17*), they succumbed to the faults from which they had so recently escaped (*verses 17, 19*). Moreover, each time they sank lower and lower (*verse 19b*). Cundall says: 'The voice of conscience can become dulled by successive acts of sin, and repentance can become more and more superficial until, ensnared in the character formed by a multitude of thoughts and actions, a miracle is needed to produce a genuine repentance and a seeking of the Lord with the whole heart.'[7]

The lesson for us is this. We are not simply to seek the

---

5. Cundall, p. 69.

6. Our understanding of the actual length of the period depends on chronology. The issue is debated among scholars and those interested are referred to more scholarly commentaries or dictionaries for a full discussion.

7. Cundall, p. 70.

Lord because we are in a mess and need help. Rather, we are to desire his glory above all things and come right back to him. Only then is there any hope of permanent blessing in the future. Or is a miracle already needed to rouse us from our selfish preoccupation with our own distress?

In addition to this, this section teaches the need to re-learn spiritual warfare (*3:1-6*). Three reasons for the continued presence of enemies in the land are given in this passage. As a result of their failure, the people were being punished (*verses 20f.*). In addition to this, the enemies remained to test their faithfulness (*verse 22*). But there is a final reason. Enemies remained to teach the new generations the art of warfare (*3:2*).

Joshua and his contemporaries had not overcome the nations of the land by their own power or earthly weapons (as the defeat of Jericho and defeat by Ai showed). Rather it was the miraculous help of the Lord to a people utterly dependent upon him and obedient to him that had brought success. It was this lesson that the people needed to relearn. Only then would the selfish religion that characterised them have its power broken.

If there is one lesson in this passage it is this. Spiritual battles are won in no other way (compare 3:10; 6:34; 9:23; 11:29; 13:25; 14:6,19; 15:14,19 with Zechariah 4:6). As we labour and seek to be obedient in all things we look to him who, alone, can effect an increase.

This is a solemn passage in a solemn book. And yet it is encouraging too! For it is the merciful Lord who was ordering the Israelites' way (as ours) even in defeat. This section is full of God's acts of righteous vengeance against the people who had forsaken his covenant: the Lord was provoked **to anger** (*verse 12*), **the hand of the LORD was against them** (*verse 15*) and **the LORD was very angry** (*verse 20*). Yet all this is admixed with his mercy: **the LORD raised up judges** (*verse 16*) and he **had compassion on them** (*verse 18*). His hand of wrath was mixed with mercy to the end that the people might come back to the place of blessing and success. May we learn the lesson well and not fail his mercy.

Sadly, it failed to work for the Israelites. Forbidden marriage contracts were made, idolatrous worship adopted (*3:5,6*) and the people **refused to give up their evil practices and stubborn ways** (*verse 19*).

Questions:

1. 'Count your blessings, name them one by one'. As you reflect upon God's mercies to you, what effect can you detect that they have had upon your faithfulness (or lack of it)? How might this passage apply to your situation?

2. In the light of this passage, what can you and I learn about the nature and the progress of sin? In what ways does your experience confirm the truth of this passage?

3. What does this passage teach us about the relationship between blessing and God's approval of us? How might your answer be relevant to situations known to you?

Introduction to 3:7-16:31

In 3:7-16:31 the cycle of sin, judgement, deliverance and blessing introduced in 2:16ff. is illustrated by a series of examples. Thirteen 'deliverers' are described: six are very briefly mentioned (Shamgar, Tola, Jair, Ibzan, Elon and Abdon), but seven of them have their activities described more fully.

The story is designed to provide a somewhat repetitive and depressing story and we should not fail to notice this! The Book of Judges was written to emphasise the fact that God's people seldom or but slowly learn the folly of deserting him. Repetition only goes to show how slow we sometimes are to learn and, at the same time, emphasises how vital is the lesson.

While the previous observations suggest the nature of the basic framework for the central chapters of the Book of Judges, it is important that we do not miss the distinctive features in each of the stories. Thus, as we proceed, we shall concentrate upon the distinctive lessons of each episode in the story. But though we shall do this, we must not forget the overall message of this central section of the book.

3:7-5:31 is the first part of this large, central section of the Book of Judges. If the chronology which is preferred by the present author is adopted, these chapters cover a period of over 200 years from about 1435 to 1229 BC. So the story begins shortly after the death of Joshua (who died about 1442) and proceeds to recount three separate periods of oppression and deliverance. These are:

i) the subjection to Cushan-Rishathaim which was brought to an end by Othniel (*3:7-11*).

ii) the Moabite and Philistine incursions into the land against which Ehud (*3:12-30*) and Shamgar (*3:31*) rebelled.

iii) the oppression by Jabin, king of Hazor from whom the Israelites were delivered by Deborah and Barak (*chapters 4, 5*).

3:7-11: The Cycle Begins

Any visitor to Palestine today is very quickly made aware of the vital importance of water to the economy of the modern state of Israel. Tour guides emphasise the importance of drinking little and often to avoid dehydration. A bus tour around the country emphasises how important modern irrigation schemes are to agricultural success. Jerusalem itself rests on the edge of the barren desert wastelands of the southern part of the country.

It was ever so! And living on the knife edge between plenty and want (depending on whether the rains came at the right time), the ancient inhabitants of Canaan had developed a religion designed to ensure that drought was averted. Modern students would describe the religion by the term 'sympathetic magic'. So, if the worshipper desired a particular blessing from his god he would try to draw his god's attention to his need by doing something designed to remind the god of the need. The prophets of Baal tried to remind Baal of their need for fire to descend from heaven by cutting themselves so that blood (red like fire) would run down their bodies (1 Kings 18). It was hoped that this might encourage Baal to send fire down.

Similarly, when the Canaanites sought good flocks they would go to their shrines and have sex with the pagan shrine prostitutes, in the hope that Baal might fertilise the land. This is the background to the mention of **the Baals** and **the Asherahs** (the female partners of the Baals) in verse 7.

The Israelites found Baalism a constant temptation. On the one hand they were called to simply trust God for their needs and humbly look to him who had done so much for them. On the other hand, faced with the possibility of ruin, there was always the temptation to feel that it might be worth trying something else to ensure their well-being.

Moreover, the situation could be looked at another way. It was true, of course, that the Lord had done some spectacular things in the nation's history. But in Canaan their needs were rather different. Here it was not spectacular interventions in history that were required but the provision of day to day necessities. Perhaps the local gods were more adept at meeting these sort of needs?

Either way, Israel's error was, as Michael Wilcock puts it, 'the classic sin of preferring the local gods to her own God'[8]: the sin, that is, of centring her life on the values of the world around her, and of assuming that in practice they are more important and valid than the Lord is.

Such apostasy began (and begins) when the people **forgot the Lord** (*verse 7*). This is a significant phrase. God's people seldom take a decisive step and reject the Lord. If they did, it would be so much more easy to spot and so much easier to handle pastorally. But it is not usually like that. No deliberate decision is taken to exchange the Lord for the gods of this world. Rather a gradual decline takes place, often so imperceptible that those who are on such a path do not even notice what is happening. Little by little the Lord has a smaller and smaller place in the lives of such people and at length he is 'forgotten' for all practical purposes; and apostasy is complete and the individual or nation conforms to the prevailing world-view. This can happen, of course, even while the Lord is still, at least nominally, worshipped, and this is what happened to

8. Wilcock, p. 37.

the people of Israel shortly after the death of Joshua. Only by care and diligence can we ensure the same does not happen to us: after all consider how often this has been true over the years in the churches we know. We surely cannot rest content when others who once walked with us have forgotten the Lord.

One of the most graphic passages in the Old Testament is found in Deuteronomy 27 and 28. There the Israelites were commanded to divide into two groups upon the slopes of the two mountains, Ebal and Gerizim. One group were to shout out the blessings of faithful obedience to God's covenant with his people. The others were to respond by calling out the curses that the Lord would bring upon those who failed him. There God had promised the very things the Canaanite gods claimed to provide if his people were faithful (*28:3-6*), but he had threatened destruction at the hands of their enemies if they failed (see especially *28:20ff.*).

All too quickly the people aroused **the anger of the LORD** (*verse 8*). Their first enemy arose from the north. **Aram Naharaim** means 'Syria of the two rivers' and probably refers to the Mesopotamian territories between the Tigris and the Euphrates. Because of the Arabian Desert lying east of the Jordan, all the ancient trade routes from Mesopotamia circumscribed a great loop north and west before entering the Jordan rift valley and sweeping south. Hence **Cushan-Rishathaim** was the first of many to attack the people of God from the north and he may well have been the head of an ancient 'super-power'. His name as given here actually means 'Cushan of the double wickedness' and is the sort of name oppressed peoples grimly give in jest to their enemies. This being the case, it hints at the severity of the sufferings the people experienced under his rule. Indeed, the cruelty of the peoples from the north was a by-word in the ancient world.

Remarkably, we are told that it was the Lord who **sold** the people into Cushan's hands. This emphasises a vital biblical truth. God would sooner suffer reproach than an apostate people. When God's people suffer disgrace he can become a reproach among the ungodly. But, this passage emphasises, the Lord would sooner have this than that his holiness is 'endangered' by his people. When the people **did evil** (*verse 7*, and see *verse 12*) the Lord punished them and allowed them to be trampled under foot by other nations (and let us not forget it) who saw the victory as being from their gods.

Doubtless the Israelites had not yet sunk to the level of the peoples around them. But they had declined from righteousness – the only thing that could outwardly distinguish themselves as the Lord's. Thus, he sold his people into slavery to other nations and their gods (*verse 8*). As their benevolent master he had every right. As their covenant God it was his duty to those who had 'torn up' the covenant agreement.

Today both individuals and churches are too often in precisely this situation. In unrighteousness we find ourselves powerless and forsaken by the Lord.

It is often assumed that when they **cried out to the LORD** (*verse 9*), the people were responding to their suffering in repentance. However, Davis suggests that this was not the case. He notes that when the phrase is used elsewhere 'the emphasis remains on the condition of distress rather than on any expression of repentance'.[9] Thus, he suggests, when the Lord raised up a saviour for Israel, 'he was responding to their misery rather than their sorrow, to their pain rather than their penitence.'[10] In this way the Lord's mercy, even for a sinful people, is exalted. The deliverance was sheer grace!

We have already met **Othniel** (see *1:11-15*). Presumably now an aged man, he was none the less raised up by the Lord to venture forth against the Lord's enemies and secure victory and a lasting peace of **forty years** (*verse 11*). For this task he was equipped by the **Spirit of the Lord** who **came upon him** (*verse 10*). Thus a good man was raised up and, equipped with the resources necessary (which outran all human ones), he was able to deliver God's people. Would the lesson be learnt by Israel?

Questions:

1. What are the equivalent of the Baals and the Asherahs in today's world? In what way have they exercised a fatal fascination over the church?

2. What lessons might you personally learn from the information we are given about Othniel in this passage?

3. Are there situations today that you can identify where God seems to be allowing his own name to be ill-spoken of, rather than be seen as the God of a sinful people? What might we learn from this?

---

9. Davis, p. 50.
10. *op. cit.*

31

3:12-31: Saved by the Unexpected

These verses describe Israel's bondage and deliverance from an enemy from the east (**Moab**) and one from the west (**the Philistines**). It is surely not without significance that Israel's first three enemies come from different points of the compass. The point should not be lost on us. When we fail to live in trusting obedience we are surrounded by potential enemies! In fact, as we shall see, Judges even goes on to speak of the enemy within (*chapters 4, 5*).

While reflecting on these enemies it is interesting to notice how different they were. Cushan, as we have seen, was probably a great king. The Phoenicians (Philistines) were also a powerful race; though scarcely in the same league. Jabin and Eglon were only local petty rulers. But the Israelites fell before them all!

Sadly, all too often departure from the Lord means that we are powerless both morally and spiritually. Apostasy is quickly seen in a decline in morality. This is inevitable. As we show less concern for the Lord we will be less interested in his standards and, therefore, will be more quickly ensnared by sin. Spiritually, too, the people knew no success or blessing. How could they? And how can we?

We note that apostasy is followed by increasingly harsh punishment. First it was eight years (*verse 8*), then eighteen (*verse 14*). In 4:3 it will be twenty years. This shows two things. The people may have been slower to turn to the Lord. Or, perhaps more likely, the Lord found it necessary to punish his people more and more severely in order to seek to awaken them to the realities of the situation.

This point was surely pressed home here when the people became subject to **Moab**, and the **Ammonites and**

Amalekites (*verse 13*). These three nations had arisen as a result of faithlessness among those who were among the 'family of God' (see Genesis 19:30-38; 36:9-12). That the people of God were now subjected to utterly godless peoples should have brought them up short with a start. When we are powerless before the attacks of apostates, do we feel the rebuke we should?

Nevertheless there is another side to the story here. It describes the people and the tactics God uses. It is instructive to compare the three saviours of Israel described in this passage.

As we have seen, **Othniel** was a senior citizen. It seems almost certain that he had known Egypt as a child, that he had known the wilderness wanderings, and that he had, probably, become a leader among the Israelites in Canaan (this seems to explain the note about him in 1:11-15).

Ehud was a 'handicapped' person: quite literally, since he was left-handed (*verse 15*). Both in Israel then, and in many societies today, this was regarded as a disadvantage. But cunning, brave Ehud (see again below) was able to turn his disability into a strength.

Shamgar may well have been a Canaanite: his name and home town/family name suggest this (more scholarly works offer the reasons for this conclusion). Perhaps he was a recent convert to the Lord. Stirred by the contradiction between God's promises and his experience and concern for the honour of the Lord he took up any available instrument and wielded it for the Lord (the **ox-goad**, verse 31, could be made into a vicious eight-foot long weapon!). Perhaps the Philistines had made this necessary by disarming the Israelites (compare 1 Samuel 13:19-22).

The lesson from all this is obvious. The Lord will use anyone for his glory: he will use all those who seek his honour above everything else. Through them he will establish his righteousness (*verse 10*, this is what the term 'judge' implies). Through them he will win victories. There are none too old, too green, too handicapped to work for him! Under his blessing God can use us all whatever our personalities and gifts: after all he made us the way we are and called us to work for his victory!

Our warfare is spiritual. We are called to establish the kingdom and the glory of Jesus. As a result of this we are not called to armed resistance, but we are called to put on the whole armour of God and go forth to undertake spiritual warfare. May we not prove apostate and faithless but find in the Spirit of Jesus our strength and victory!

There are some further details in this passage that are worth noticing before we conclude our study. **Eglon** seems to have established his base in Jericho, **the City of Palms** (*verse 13*). What an irony! The place where Israel had experienced its greatest victory in the conquest of the land was now occupied by the enemy and oppressor.

A further irony is that Ehud was presumably chosen to be the envoy of Israel precisely because he was a cripple and could not, therefore, be seen as a threat. The Hebrew text makes this more apparent than English versions by telling us that Ehud could not use his right hand. He was left-handed of necessity! And surely a left-handed cripple is no threat to anyone? Note that there may be a further irony, in that Ehud was a **Benjamite** (*verse 15*); literally, from the tribe of the 'son of the right hand'.

Some commentators make a great deal of the fact that

there is no mention of the Holy Spirit as equipping Ehud for his saving role. Here, it is suggested, God allows human efforts to triumph. For some expositors this helps resolve the embarrassment that they feel about God giving a **deliverer** who didn't fight by the Marquis of Queensberry's rules (*verse 15*) !

But we can be unduly squeamish. Life in this world is not conducted within a sanitised environment. A sinful world is a world which is messy. And most of us work with some sort of definition of a 'just war' where sometimes the ends justify the means. However, this passage tells us that God is willing to get his hands dirty (very dirty!) in order to effect the gracious salvation of his people. What a joy that is!

Graeme Auld describes this story as 'delightful'! That may not be our opinion, but surely the details of this story are described with a view to making Israel laugh again. How is the mighty oppressor overthrown! And what a victory ensued! Again a phenomenal number of the enemy were slain (**ten thousand**, *verse 29* and see *1:4*) and a period of extended peace (**eighty years** or two generations, *verse 30*) followed. How gracious is our God!

Questions:

1. Is it ever right to deceive others or lie? Compare this passage with Exodus 1:19-20 and give reasons for your conclusions.

2. What comfort can be drawn from this passage and its

description of God getting his 'hands dirty'? How might the lessons apply to your life today?

3. Reflect on the way this passage exalts God's grace. What response ought you and I to offer to the revelation of God given here?

4. This passage shows that God often works in unexpected ways. He saves his people in unexpected ways and by unexpected people. What might we learn from this? Are there any limits which God places upon himself when doing the 'novel thing'? What are they?

4:1-5:31: Saved By Two Women!

This glorious deliverance of the people of God by Deborah and Barak brings to an end the first cycle of the stories about the judges (*3:7-5:31*).

The details of the battle described here are not easy to reconstruct and there are not a few scholars quick to point out apparent contradictions between the two accounts of victory in chapters 4 and 5. However, when we bear in mind that the second account is a poem and that poetry, by definition, is less concerned with literal factual truth than with seeking to capture the spirit and the emotions associated with what is described, the problems evaporate! Moreover, it is questionable whether the disparities are any greater than the variations between two people who give their testimony of the same event. There are no irreconcilable contradictions. Happily, moreover, none of this inhibits our general understanding of the passage nor its application.

The time came when **Ehud died** and, with the external restraint taken away, Israel reverted to her true character and **did evil in the eyes of the LORD** (*4:1*). Davis notes: 'There is something wrong with religion when its degree of fidelity depends solely on outside pressures, influences and leadership'.[11] However, this fundamental weakness will characterise Israel throughout this book. Israel's faith was never more than skin-deep. It failed to become a religion of the heart. That this is the issue here is demonstrated by Deborah's words in 5:31 when she speaks of true believers as **they who love you**. This verse is crucial to an understanding of the present section for it describes the Lord's purpose for his people as one in which their glory and power increases like the sun to its zenith. Such a defeat of his enemies then becomes the Lord's own vindication: a fact which Deborah clearly recognised in her song (*5:3, 10f.*). God's desire is his own glory seen in the victory and honour of his own people. We need to rediscover this optimistic perspective which pervades the Scriptures. It is sadly lacking today and Christians sometimes glory in their reproach. Not so Deborah, who recognised that she needed waking up out of such a dishonouring and slothful attitude!

Yet we must not fail to notice that God would sooner deny his glory than have those who own his name fail to live for him alone and love him above all else.

What then was the failure of the people at this point? The key word is **again** (*4:1*). Wickedness, as Wilcock notes, is desperately unoriginal and in Israel's case it varied only in that it got worse.[12] Once again, the people were

---

11. Davis, p. 73. 12. Wilcock, p. 52.

guilty of apostasy; **they chose new gods** (*5:8*). But this apostasy was the result of unbelief. Failure to trust God and his word forced them to seek substitutes, other means to secure their well-being. We are no different: we often look to programmes and techniques rather than to the Lord and his Word. The root of such an attitude may lie in a failure to believe that God can do anything more than we can achieve for ourselves. It can also be found in wanting guarantees beyond the Word itself. Some think that that was Barak's problem (*4:8*). So, they argue, while there is a proper sense of inadequacy when faced with a responsibility given to us by the Lord (compare 2 Corinthians 3:5, 6), this was not Barak's problem as the following judgement (even if mildly expressed by a gentle God) makes plain (*4:9*). Others, however, suggest that this is unlikely. Wilcock, for example, notes that Hebrews 11:32 commends Barak's faith (not that of Deborah or Jael). Moreover, he is willing to go, if the conditions are met. This is not downright disobedience! So 'Barak's missing the honour of killing Sisera, is not necessarily a rebuke – it is just as likely to be a plain statement of fact'[13] (obscured by the NIV translation). In the light of this it is perhaps best to see Barak's faith as weak but genuine and that he was seeking the assurances that most of us look for when God calls us to step out boldly for him. That Barak was willing to step out is all to his credit in the circumstances since he was being invited to lead a small band of peasants, without weapons (*5:8*), against a crack professional army of enormous size (note the repetition of **nine hundred iron chariots** in *4:3, 13*). Small wonder the writer to the He-

---

13. Wilcock, p. 63.

brews sees him as a champion of the faith!

However, if this was not Barak's problem, it certainly had been that of the people as a whole. For over **twenty years** (*4:3*) the people had done nothing; despite the fact that God had promised them the land occupied by their enemies and that his glory and their blessing were at stake. We can sympathise with their reasoning. What use would the 10,000 Israelites be against the enemy's 900 chariots? But Paul could warn against seeking to live by appearances and not faith (2 Corinthians 5:7): it is a fault to which we are all inevitably prone. But we must recognise it for the sin it is and place ourselves, once and for all, under the Word of God: under its promises and revelation of the character of God and under the evidence of God's faithfulness in the past.

Interestingly, the fact that it was **Jabin, a king of Canaan, who reigned in Hazor** (*4:2*) should have given Israel pause for thought. Not only had God promised time and again that he would expel the Canaanites from the land but a former Jabin had been routed (as Joshua 11:10f. tells us). The situation was clearly not hopeless if God was on his people's side!

This passage emphasises, however, the desperate consequences that result from a failure in God's people to trust him. They lost their honour, and the name and favour of the Lord was greatly obscured. They were subjected to war, weakness and servitude. They were **cruelly oppressed** (*4:3*); a word used, as Jordan notes[14], of the Egyptian bondage in Exodus 1:13-14. Communications were disrupted, agriculture affected. In sum, they were in

---

14. Jordan, p. 74.

a sorry mess (*5:6f.*). Davis says, 'Times were so bad folks couldn't even travel safely – they had to take the back roads because thieves and thugs freeloaded on the highways. Israel was totally defenceless, having neither warriors (*verse 7a*) nor weapons (*verse 8b*) ...'[15] When faith goes out the window the same is always true: far from securing what little we have (the usual motive), we lose even that! God's people are not called to defend ground already held but to go out to win fresh victories and possessions.

Humanly speaking the odds against the Christian and the church are always too great. Barak, as we have seen, recognised that in his own situation. However, we are not to use the 'realities of the situation' in such a way as to overthrow faith. There is a place for realism and common sense among believers: but it is not here! God had spoken: **The LORD, the God of Israel, commands you: Go**...(*4:6*). Living in obedient faith, Barak soon discovered that the battle was not his because **the LORD routed Sisera** (*4:15*). Barak did not have to fight for victory: all he had to do was to pursue a fleeing enemy (*4:16*)! As to the battle itself, Barak is not mentioned! What then did those fearsome chariots mean to the Lord and those who believed in him? Indeed, as the sequel pointedly shows (*4:17-22* and *5:24-27*), a lone believing woman was sufficient to break the power of the Canaanites once and for ever. Never again did they constitute a threat to the people of Israel. They were an enemy routed once and for ever.

How slow we are to learn the same lessons. The hymnwriter says:

---

15. Davis, p. 84.

Soldiers of Christ arise,
and put your armour on,
strong in the strength which God supplies
through His eternal Son.

This attitude has always accompanied the expansion of the church.

The Bible is full of ironic humour. This is evident here. The Israelites were tempted, as we have already seen, to look to nature gods to meet their daily needs. Hence Baal was often depicted as the god of the thunderstorm. Here Barak (which means 'thunderbolt') was assisted by what appears to be a thunderstorm (see, especially the description of its results in *5:20ff.*) to overthrow the Canaanites who worshipped the 'thunder god'. As far as the Canaanites were concerned the only thing that **thundered** for them were the **horses' hoofs**; in retreat! Perhaps we are intended to grasp at this point that, as Jordan puts it, all 'pagan religion is a cheap and perverted [we might add, powerless] copy of the truth'.[16]

A faithful leadership is a great blessing. 5:2 and 9 make it clear that responsible, believing leadership can transform a cowering people into the horde who rushed down Mount Tabor to victory. **When the princes in Israel take the lead ... the people willingly offer themselves ....** The world, of course, knows this well. A people are seldom more visionary and confident than their leaders – those who are expected to show them an example. Thus, if the lessons of these two chapters are to be learnt by all of us, they are to be especially carefully considered by those who are or aspire to being leaders. Leaders are to lead!

---

16. Jordan, p. 91.

These two chapters also introduce to us the tragedy of the spectator. Some, but not all, of those who were available to fight for the victory of the Lord took up arms. Some, however, did not respond. In trans-Jordan there was a great deal of talk and **searching of heart** (*5:15,16*), but the needs of their flocks of sheep took precedence over the 'flock' of Israel. Self-interest took precedence over seeking God's glory and obedience to his command. A similar situation pertained in **Dan** (*5:17*). They had developed a 'nice little line' in trading; to abandon profit-making for obedience to the call of God's prophetess was a non-starter! Whether farmers or merchants they stood aloof from the battle. There were even those who, with success surrounding them, remained aloof. We do not know where **Meroz** was (*5:23*) but all the indications of the context suggest a location near where the battle took place.

This is so often the tragic truth about the Lord's children. Lazy, self-centred, concerned not for the Lord's glory but only their own security, and critical and aloof even when blessing is evident, they invite God's curse.

As we noted in our comments on 2:1-5 **the angel of the LORD** first appears in Genesis 16. In this and all subsequent appearances the angel is identified with God but as being distinct from God. Many conclude that he is a pre-incarnation appearance of Christ. Whether or not this is so, the presence of the angel indicates that this is no message mediated through a prophet. Failure here by Meroz invited a curse from God's own lips!

Before we leave these two chapters we cannot but fail to note that this is a very odd story! **Deborah** is both a judge and a **prophetess** who **was leading Israel at that**

time (*4:4*). Yet, paradoxically, though scarcely any others of the judges are portrayed as 'the wise, mature, godly person that she is'[17], she does not stand at the centre of the story.

Then, while the words of her prophecy **the LORD will hand Sisera over to a woman** (*4:9*) lead us to expect her to take centre stage, it is Jael who is described as the **most blessed of women** (*5:24*) for the part she played in Sisera's death.

But this is not all! *Jael* is celebrated in glowing, almost gloating, terms as the saviour of Israel (*5:24-27*; see, especially, *verse 27*). However, commentators are not slow to point out her 'sins'. Jordan is not untypical. He mentions insubordination to her husband in breaking a treaty he had made (*4:17*), breaking the household treaty with Jabin (*4:17*), deception (*4:18*), lying (*4:18*), violating the laws of hospitality (*4:18-21*) and murder (*4:21*).[18] The list is not exhaustive! Klein suggests that the fact that the Lord is not mentioned in 5:24-27 implies disapproval[19]; blessed among women she may be, but not by the Lord. In response, Jordan may overstate when he says, 'we cannot escape the clear approval of God for Jael's actions'.[20] However, we are at least faced with a question which, as Wilcock notes, 'will press on us increasingly: how does God's concern with the thing he wants done relate to his concern with the motives and the methods of the person who does it?'[21]

Possibly, those of us who have never experienced cruel oppression are more squeamish than we ought to be when

---

17. Wilcock, p. 62. 18. Jordan, p. 87. 19. Klein, p. 45.
20. Jordan, p. 87. 21. Wilcock, p. 61.

faced with the messiness of life in this world and God's actions in it. Sisera, the agent of Jabin, **cruelly oppressed** Israel (*4:3*) and probably enjoyed raping captive Israelite girls (**a girl or two for each man**, *5:30*). He was, as Davis puts it, 'not exactly Mr Clean'.[22]

The mystery, however, continues. Israel was living in the midst of a male dominated world. What are we to make of the fact that Deborah started the ball rolling which Jael so startlingly concluded 'while God was orchestrating the piece'[23] as Wilcock so effectively expresses it?

For it was God who took on the gods of Canaan, as Deborah realised (*5:2-5*). It was he who was in control, even while his people were being circumstantially led to the point where they sought him in their distress (*5:6-8*). He was leading the armies of Israel (*5:9-13*) ... so the song continues. All was his doing. And, finally, before him the Canaanite 'confidence is seen as an illusion'[24]. For those with eyes to see it are those **who love you** who will be **like the sun when it rises in its strength** (*5:31*).

The poet, William Cowper, could say, 'God moves in a mysterious way his wonders to perform'. It was ever so! Thus, our passage concludes with the celebration of God's salvation, achieved by such unlikely methods and which lasted for at least a generation (**forty years**, *5:31*).

---

22. Davis, p. 79.
23. Wilcock, p. 64.
24. *Ibid.*, p. 66.

Questions:

1. What does this passage teach about the qualities we should look for in our leaders? To what extent do these qualities match up with those things for which we usually look? What lessons might we learn from the disparity?

2. Trace the activity of God through the variety of situations described in these two chapters. What implications should these facts have for us when we view our own circumstances or those in the world around us?

3. Look again at 4:8f.. When do you think it is appropriate to test God's call?

4. Look at 5:13-23 and the different responses people made to the call to stand up and fight for the Lord. Can you think of parallels in the church or your own life?

6:1-40: Grace For the Stubborn and Timid

This chapter begins the second cycle of stories about the judges (*6:1-10:5*) and, in particular, describes in considerable detail the call of Gideon and his early steps as the leader the Lord had appointed to deliver Israel. Indeed, as we shall see, this is the particular contribution of this chapter to the Book of Judges. Other judges simply appear on the scene. Here we are given a glimpse into the background story: the making of a faithful man of God.

This second period of the judges lasted less than 100 years. In that time there was, apparently, only **seven years** of chastisement (*verse 1*). But the misery wrought by the judgement of God described in this chapter (especially in verses 1-6) far surpassed that of previous stripes. Indeed, there is evidence of God's increasing impatience with the people; he did not 'sell them' but **gave them into the hands of the Midianites** (*verse 1*). This time the enemy came from the east. They were traditional enemies of Israel; 'nomads, scavengers ... they had no culture and no home, but wandered from place to place, robbing and pillaging.'[25] Allied with the **Amalekites**, a people who were a by-word for cynical cruelty in Bible times, and **other eastern peoples** (*verse 3*) they constituted an appalling threat. Thus, here the Israelites were obliged to take refuge in **mountain clefts, caves and strongholds** (*verse 2*) gathering together what few possessions they had as year after year **like a swarm of locusts** (*verse 5*) the enemy stripped the land of all those things vital to the ongoing life of a peasant economy. Innumerable enemies were sent, as Wilcock notes, 'as a punishment for the rejection of innumerable mercies.'[26]

Effective threshing has to be undertaken in the open and where there is a breeze. So severe was the situation, however, that Gideon is first introduced to us **threshing wheat** of such meagre quantities and in such dangerous conditions that he was doing it in a small, airless **winepress** (*verse 11*)! The very existence of the people was, therefore, seriously threatened by the danger of famine (the story of Ruth probably fits in here).

25. Jordan, p. 115. 26. Wilcock, p. 78.

This chapter teaches that there is a sorrow that falls short of true repentance (*verses 6-10*). In their extremity the people **cried out to the LORD for help** (*verse 6*). But there is that despairing seeking of God that seeks him, not for himself, but for needed blessing. Even today, people will often become very religious in times of want, but once these needs are met they turn back to their previous infidelity. This appears to have been the problem with the Israelites. Thus, first of all, the Lord sent not blessing but an unnamed prophet. Davis says, 'That would be like a stranded motorist calling a garage for assistance and the garage sending a philosopher instead of a mechanic!'[27] But Israel needed to relearn several things: they needed to re-learn their history of salvation (*verses 7-9*) and to give attention to God's commands to them (*verse 10*). Thus the prophet was sent to awaken the people to the real reason for their distress: to remind them of God's ability to help but also of his exclusive claim to them.

The learning of this lesson marks the difference between a true and counterfeit believer. The counterfeit believer is selfish and thinks only of his or her needs and how they can be met by the service of God. The true believer delights in the Lord and willingly obeys his demands, thinking first of him.

But we also learn of the nearness of the Lord to his erring people (especially *verses 11ff.*). There is something rather marvellous about this story. The people were in a desperate state. They sought the Lord, but incorrectly. Yet the Lord did not wait for them to come to a more true repentance. There is no evidence that the prophet's minis-

27. Davis, p. 92.

try had any effect; Gideon appears to have known nothing about his message and by the time the Book of Judges was written there was only some vague awareness that 'someone' had said something! Yet God, who is a God of kindness and mercy, met them, even in their half-heartedness, and took the initiative to bring them back to himself. So the **angel of the LORD** reappears (*verse 11*).

As we saw in 2:1-5 the 'Angel' was the fullest and most intimate manifestation of the Lord himself before the incarnation of his Son. Thus, appearing to Gideon in this way, he emphasised his nearness to the people, even in their rebellion! The Lord who had walked with Adam and Eve in the Garden of Eden was ready to commune with his erring people and to restore them to himself. Moreover, it was the Angel who had fought with the people against their enemies in the past (Joshua 5:13). This fact surely was to be a source of great strength to Gideon.

All this is unspeakably marvellous. We fail the Lord. So often our labours for him are half-hearted and we seek him so slothfully. How can we expect to come again to the place of blessing? For us, as for ancient Israel, the lesson is the same: he will bring us there. Our most halting and hesitating steps will speedily be accompanied by his own supporting arm!

We noted above that this chapter is distinctive in the way it describes, in detail, the early stages of Gideon's call and response. Thus we are told, first of all, about the call of Gideon (*verses 12-16*). In many respects this call parallels those of Moses and Joshua; though Gideon seems to require more convincing of God's presence and purposes than they did. In view of the immediately preceding events and the less dramatic nature of the encounter we can, perhaps, understand this!

At first sight Gideon does not seem a very likely 'winner', hidden away in the winepress. But the Lord sees him not as he is but as what he will become; a **mighty warrior** (*verse 12*). Gideon is not altogether impressed. It is all very well for this stranger (not immediately recognised by Gideon) to mouth the words **the LORD is with you** (*verse 12*), but such claims (expanded in verse 14!) don't seem to tie up with reality. After all, Gideon cynically responds, God doesn't seem the same God today who accomplished the **wonders that our fathers told us about** (*verse 13*). Moreover, there are practical problems to overcome; **my clan is the weakest in Manasseh, and I am the least in my family** (*verse 15*). This seems to have been a genuine reservation; later the Ephraimites (who considered themselves 'top dogs' were to complain to Gideon, *8:1ff.*). Gideon might well ask, 'Could a leader from a small group in despised Manasseh gain support?'

In response to this the Lord reminds Gideon of the only two things that count. First of all, he himself will empower Gideon (*verse 14* and compare *verse 34*) and, secondly, he will guarantee his presence (*verse 16*, see Psalm 23:4). When this is the case the mighty enemy will seem as though they are a single weak assailant.

We need to learn these lessons. God has called each of us to a life of service and victory. We might seem unlikely candidates for such a high calling. Moreover, there are difficulties in the way (wherever we are and whatever the task we are called to do: howsoever humble), and there is the temptation to doubt that the God of the past could ever be the same for us. But, as for Gideon, the same is true for us. He who has called is the One who equips and guarantees his victorious presence.

Sometimes, of course, the Lord seems to be calling us to a totally unexpected course of action. Then we need to be sure that it is, indeed, he who is calling. That was true with Gideon. By now he seems to have guessed who his visitor is! So he seeks some guarantees that God is truly in fellowship with him (and the people).

In war-ravaged Israel, Gideon invites his visitor to a lavish feast (*verses 17-18*). Since an **ephah** was a large enough vessel to hold a person (Zechariah 5:7), Gideon provides a baker's-store amount of bread for his guest! Moreover, bearing in mind that **sheep, cattle and donkeys** (*verse 4*) had all been commandeered by the eastern hordes, **a young goat** must have been worth a small fortune (*verse 19*). More significant than the munificence of Gideon's feast are, however, two other factors. First of all, to offer and receive a meal in Bible times was an offer and an acceptance of friendship. Secondly, these particular items were those associated with the peace offering (see, especially Leviticus 7). Thus, by sharing this meal/sacrifice God confirmed himself (*verses 17-21*), especially in the matter wherein Gideon needed the greatest reassurance (*verses 22-24*). He wanted an assurance that the Lord truly was in alliance (one of the meanings of **peace** in the Old Testament) with him. That confirmation was given and Gideon was ready for action......well, not quite!

For, next, we are introduced to his first hesitating steps in the way of believing discipleship. And how like us Gideon proved to be! Gideon could never hope to deliver

God's people unless he himself demonstrated his willingness to obey the Lord despite the cost and danger, and unless a change of heart could be effected in the people.

We should not miss the point in verse 25! 'Next God will tell Gideon to kill one of the few bulls left in the land,' notes Jordan, who then adds that when 'fellowship with God is restored, reformation must begin immediately'[28]. A clear break with Baalism had to be made; the symbols of Baal worship (the **altar** and the **Asherah pole**) had to be **cut down** (*verse 25*) and a **proper** (*verse 26*) sanctuary to the Lord put in its place. The powerlessness of Baalism was to be demonstrated by using the hewn Asherah pole as firewood for the Lord's offering!

It is easy to criticise Gideon for being **afraid** (*verse 27*) and doing what he was commanded at **night**. But, as Davis notes: 'Did God tell him to do it by day? Did God tell him he couldn't be afraid? Or did God simply tell him to do it? Evidently, obedience was essential and heroism optional.'[29]

Gideon's first steps (he **did as the Lord told him**) were rewarded by the Lord (*verse 27*) in the first glimmerings of faith in Joash his father (*verses 28ff.*), and then, apparently, the people, who soon proved willing to follow him (*verse 34*). Thus, Gideon was strengthened for his life's work. He was no longer alone! Jordan notes of this scenario that, 'The first to rally to his side were the Abiezrites, his own home town! All those men who had seen little Gideon as a child, now follow him as their leader. This required a monumental work of grace.'[30] But what

---

28. Jordan, p. 122f.   29. Davis, p. 98.
30. Jordan, p. 127.

an encouragement it would have been for Gideon to find family and friends supporting him!

Yet Gideon still had to wrestle with his temperament and the magnitude of the task to which he had been called. He still needed props for his faith (*verses 34-40*). The desire for a sign was not evidence of unbelief, but of a weak faith struggling for assurance in the face of the great task that lay ahead. Perhaps the requests were symbolic. Did the first 'sign' indicate that the Lord would once again refresh his people? Did the second indicate that the Lord would do this despite the fact that others seemed to be flourishing and blessed? We cannot be sure. What we do know is that in the sequel Gideon sought no more signs, even though the Lord pared down his army to 300 men! He had learnt to trust the Lord and to rely upon his Word alone.

There is a remarkable tenderness in the Lord's preparation of Gideon. God knew his man, as he knows us. Gideon was 'diffident, modest and shy'[31] and God recognised that Gideon could not arrive 'overnight' at maturity. Weakness along the way would need to be met and Gideon strengthened for the realities of the battle and victory ahead. Little by little, like a father with a child, the Lord raised him up. Then Gideon, the man who hid in a winepress, led the people to one of their most remarkable victories: a victory which required superhuman faith in the Lord.

The same Lord leads us. Little by little he will lead our halting steps till we too are 'more than conquerors'. We are called simply to place our hands in his and he will

31. Wilcock, p. 82.

gently lead us though we be as those with young: weak and defenceless (Isaiah 40:11)!

Thus the dour Book of the Judges proves to be one of great comfort. It does not mince words with apostasy and sin. Yet it also declares the mercy and tenderness of the Lord to those who hesitatingly tip-toe back to him. Moreover, it teaches us that God can make us 'mighty warriors' (*verse 12*) too. For the resources are his and his presence will go with us! How great is our God!

'Thus,' says Wilcock, 'the scene is set, and the saviour prepared, for the confrontation between Israel and Midian in chapter 7.'[32]

Questions:

1. Recall some of the experiences which you have had where God took the initiative to restore you to himself, despite yourself. What lessons might you learn about God from such experiences?

2. List some of the characteristic marks of false and genuine repentance. How does your own spiritual life match up to the list which you have made?

3. What tasks has God called you to undertake for him? How might God's dealings with Gideon help you to step out in obedience?

4. The restoration of communion with God requires immediate steps to be taken to reformation of life. What are the 'idols' that we should sacrifice on the Lord's altar? What sort of lifestyle should characterise a reformed life?

---

32. Wilcock, p. 82.

7:1-23: Magnificent Warrior

This and the following chapter describe Gideon's victory over the Midianites and recount several of the important events in the remainder of his life. The story is fairly self-explanatory. Those elements in it which are not so obvious will be dealt with in the course of our study.

'**The LORD,**' said Gideon, '**will rule over you**' (*8:23*). In many ways this is the theme of these two chapters. This is especially true when we recognise that kingship in the Bible is not merely a status but describes actions which demonstrate the reality of the claim to such a status. The rule of the Lord is no mere cipher. It is a fact for the believing to reckon with and live out. The reality of the Lord's rule is amply demonstrated here.

Moreover, the Lord delights in impossible situations. As we have noted before, God's people have a habit of believing that he can do little beyond that which they think that they can achieve for him. Such a belief is usually very depressing. Often we are 'up against it'. The future looks, inevitably, bleak and we become discouraged and depressed. If this is how we think, we need to reflect upon the story told here.

Gideon was faced with an army of 135,000 men (*8:10*). He himself had but 32,000 (*7:3*). But even this was subsequently reduced to 300! (*7:1-7*). The reason for this is given (*verse 2*): the Lord intended to show that the victory was his alone. Israel was to be in no position to **boast against me that her own strength has saved her**. Thus, we are taught that God especially delights to work when his people are in extremity! Their extremity is his opportunity. No situation is beyond him.

There may have been a wisdom about the two tests which were required of Gideon's men. Cowards are a drain upon any army. Thus, from a human point of view, we can understand the command, '**Anyone who trembles with fear may turn back**' (*verse 3*). We, too, are called to confidence in the Lord and boldness occasioned by such faith. He is the King after all. However, it is a mark of so much contemporary evangelicalism that such holy boldness is almost universally absent. There is little of Carey's confidence found among us. Yet we have the more ample ground to 'Expect great things from God' and to 'Attempt great things for God'. Jesus himself has come and demonstrated the total commitment of the Lord to us.

The second test may, perhaps, have been seen as one of preparedness and alertness (*7:4-8*). The Lord may have wished to single out those who were ready for battle, alert to seize every opportunity in faith. How often we are blind to the opportunities and how ill-prepared we often are. Yet if he is the King and we are believing, what cannot we achieve for him?

However, all this may be to read more into the text than is there (despite the popularity of this view)! In fact a 'small corps of crack troops is precisely what God does not want'.[33] Rather, the three hundred are such an inadequate group that there will be no other explanation possible than, '**I will deliver you**' (*verse 7*). Moreover, the command of verse 3 may have a lot more to do with learning obedience to God's will (compare Deuteronomy 20:8). Thus, we should focus far more upon the fact that God called Gideon to obedience and faith in the impossible.

---

33. Wilcock, p. 71.

However, we must not pass by verses 9-15. Faith and bravery often exist alongside doubts and fears. Because we are human it is with anxiety and trembling that we often venture on the Lord. He understands this! And he is ready to strengthen the failing heart. God did not rebuke Gideon but helped him to gain a greater confidence in his God.

We can imagine Gideon and his colleague **Purah** (*verses 10, 11*) creeping into the Midianite camp under cover of darkness. What they saw was enough to frighten anyone out of their wits: the army had **settled in the valley, thick as locusts** and **their camels alone could no more be counted than the sand on the seashore** (*verse 12*). Here was an invitation to abandon plans for battle and return to the mountain caves. But wait...

What did Gideon and Purah hear? A Midianite private shares a dream with a friend (*verse 13*) who immediately understands its interpretation (*verse 14*). Those of us familiar with the story can miss the point. How is it that this man has even heard of Gideon and his antecedents? What has prompted this vast horde to such anxiety as presumably is reflected in the dream and its interpretation? Odds of 450:1 on are scarcely a reason for a dream-troubled sleep! There can be no other explanation than that offered to his troops by Gideon: '**The LORD has given the Midianite camp into your hands**.' Small wonder Gideon **worshipped** (*verse 15*). Thus God encouraged Gideon. 'This,' says Jordan, 'is the love of God, dealing gently with his immature child.'[34] But do we ever get beyond such immature needs in the present life of faith? As we

---

34. Jordan, p. 134.

wrestle through by faith we should learn from this and not be ashamed of our fears but look to him who is able to garrison us in the midst of our fears and bring us to victory.

The Kingship of the Lord is vividly illustrated in the battle itself. As with Deborah and Barak, so Gideon discovered that he had to pursue a defeated enemy (*verse 21*). In the battle itself the people **each held his position**. Much work remained to be done: work that would prove utterly exhausting at times (*8:4*). But the power of the enemy had been broken before ever the people took a step. The same is true for us. The Lord Jesus has already broken Satan's power. We are called to undertake the mopping up operations. His is the kingdom, the power and the glory!

Some commentators suggest that Gideon showed tremendous skill in 'psychological warfare' in the strategy he adopted (*verses 17-21*). Thus he acted at the time of night when sleepers roused were most likely to be disorientated. A new watch would have scarcely had opportunity to adjust their eyes to the darkness. The returning watch, groping around to find their tents, might easily be mistaken for the enemy, the noise and fire might have stampeded the camels, and Gideon's feared name together with the above factors might have induced panic.

There may be some truth in all of this. However, the emphasis the text seeks to make is that the LORD **caused** the rout (*verse 22*).

And thus Gideon matures as a man of faith. As the story has proceeded, 'Out of weakness he begins to be made strong, becomes mighty in war, and puts foreign enemies to flight, as Hebrews 11:34 will phrase it.'[35]

---

35. Wilcock, p. 73.

Questions:

1. In what areas of your life might God be calling you to look to him for victory? What warnings and encouragements can you draw from this chapter?

2. Reflect upon examples known to you where opposition to God crumbled in the face of a believing people. How does this apply to situations that you or your church face now?

7:24-8:35: A Right Royal Failure!

There is something very strange about this entire section. Most of the actions that Gideon takes can be justified. And yet as one reads through the account one gets an increasing sense that all is not well. Thus, each section provokes the question, 'Was Gideon right or wrong?', and the answer is usually 'Maybe'. This is the great problem with so many of our actions; they can invariably be justified (sometimes with good theological reasons) but what, deep down, is the motive? Are they God-honouring or are our motives mixed? Or is what we say merely an excuse? Every pastor knows that this is one of the most difficult issues in pastoral care. On the surface, all may appear well or there may be only a hint that things are not quite right.

As the Midianites flee, Gideon calls for the intervention of the tribe of **Ephraim** (*7:24*). Prompt support is sought and given and the result is that **Oreb and Zeeb**, two of the ringleaders of the Midianite hordes, are captured trying to re-cross the Jordan and are put to death (*verse 25*). So far, so good.

As Judges 12:1-6 will show, Ephraim, the tribe of Joshua, considered itself the senior tribe of the Israelite confederation. Gideon was an Abiezrite ('A who?' one can hear an Ephraimite saying), but had only called in Ephraim for 'mopping-up' operations. What an indignity for the tribe who thought it should lead! So they resorted to the timeless tactic and **criticised him sharply** (*verse 1*). The fact that Gideon was obeying the Lord seemed to have passed them by, or certainly constituted a minor consideration. After all, pride was hurt!

So often this is the case at a time of blessing. The devil is very active to undermine the work of the Lord. One of the most effective ways is to divide the people of God and thus undermine their prosperity.

What do we make of Gideon's response? This was no time for infighting and there are occasions when humility is better than force. This is the course of action Gideon resolved on. He pointed out that they had captured the leaders of the Midianite federation. What was his own achievement in the light of such a magnificent catch? So, we are told, the Ephraimites' **resentment against him subsided** (*verse 3*). Or was his response symptomatic of Gideon's own sense of inadequacy emerging once again? Would firm action at this point have avoided future problems? The problem is, we do not know.

Similar questions keep re-surfacing. Weary, yet still pursuing, Gideon arrived at two Israelite village outposts, **Succoth** (*verse 5*) and **Peniel** (*verse 8*). At each, he made the **same request**, a moderate one – **bread** (but not meat). The leaders of Succoth, near as they were to the territory of the Midianites, seemed unwilling to put their head in the noose if events turned against Gideon. Referring to an ancient practice of war, the cutting off of the hands of the vanquished (*verse 6*), they refer to two of the Midianite leaders still at large – **Zebah and Zalmunna**. Without their capture, they have no intention of helping Gideon!

The response was understandable but faithless. They refused to recognise the work of God and declined to have any part in the victory of Gideon. Gideon, understandably, recognised this as evidence of apostasy. In language drawn from the vocabulary of holy war he warns the inhabitants of Succoth that he will now treat them as enemies and hence he warns, '**I will tear your flesh with desert thorns and briers**' (*verse 7*). Peniel gets a similar warning, '**I will tear down this tower**' (*verse 9*).

Victory followed (*verses 10-12*) and Gideon returned and fulfilled his dark promise (*verses 13-17*). He is able to offer his reasons: he has now captured the chieftains of whom they spoke and they had failed to help **exhausted men** (*verse 15*). If he had wanted a biblical justification he could have doubtless appealed to Deuteronomy 20:13.

Yet the language and the savagery of his action makes the reader uncomfortable; especially bearing in mind that he had needed quite some convincing and encouragement to respond to God's call himself. Klein says: 'The judge seems to have no compunction about torturing or killing those Israelites who have doubts in him, which is in sharp contrast to the treatment he received from Yahweh when Gideon was in doubt.'[36] One is tempted to ask the question, 'Does he throw his weight around with the weak and vulnerable while temporising with powerful Ephraim?'

---

36. Klein, p. 62.

Commentators disagree on their verdict. Perhaps we are meant to be confused.

This does not mean that we ought not to be challenged by the failure of these two villages. Too often Christian churches have members who seem more concerned to further their own ambitions and build up their pride than manifest grace in love and unity and in self-effacement. Too often there are those who for all their fine words do nothing to advance the Lord's cause. We need to be alerted by this part of Gideon's story. At best we are unspiritual. At worst we are strangers to the grace of God.

Equally, those of us in leadership do well not to 'throw our weight around' and fail to offer the grace and mercy to others that we have ourselves received.

Interpretation of verses 18-21 is very difficult. There are various possibilities. Is this all the language of what Soggin calls 'epic chivalry'[37] (and therefore not to be taken at face value; the fate of these men is sealed)? Or is this an implied challenge to produce these men alive? Perhaps we should choose the simple option. Gideon would have shown compassion for Zebah and Zalmunna if they had not killed his family (presumably some time prior to the events described in these chapters).

If this is the case, Gideon shows less willingness to show concern for his own people than his enemies. Moreover, the enemies of God's people were to be destroyed. Again, all this reads far more like a personal vendetta than a holy war in obedience to the Lord. While justifying Gideon's earlier actions, Jordan suggests that attempting to exonerate him here 'seems as if we are straining at a gnat

37. Soggin, p. 157.

and swallowing a camel'[38]. Earlier hesitations about his motives and approach are receiving a confirmatory nudge.

This makes one suspicious of Gideon's actions in verses 20 and 21. Getting his young (teenage?) son to do his 'dirty work' can be variously seen as an unsavoury attempt to humiliate Zebah and Zalmunna. Equally, it can be viewed as a sort of dynastic claim for **Jether**, his firstborn. 'Remember him,' the Israelites might have said when Gideon died, 'he slew Zebah and Zalmunna when he was only a slip of a lad. What an ideal judge he would make.' It is certainly difficult to see Gideon's suggestion in a God-honouring light.

The same goes for the plunder he takes (*verse 21*); **the ornaments off their camels' necks**. Viewed positively, it is simply obedience to Deuteronomy 20:14. Or is this a first step to acquiring worldly splendour to bolster his judgeship?

It is difficult to escape the conclusion that self was re-asserting itself in Gideon. Mighty in the heat of the battle, he was learning what we need to learn. It is often when the going is easier and in the day-to-day life that faithfulness to the Lord is more difficult to sustain. Christian preachers who challenge their hearers as to whether they have the resources for the heat of battle have often got it wrong. The greatest need is not when we are utterly cast upon the Lord but when power and prosperity allows us to build foundations elsewhere!

This brings us to verses 22-27. The offer of dynastic power was understandable (*verse 22*) and Gideon's response (*verse 23*) was commendable (and theologically

---

38. Jordan, p. 147.

impeccable) ... or was it? Is Gideon giving an outright, 'No' or is he saying 'Yes, though you ought to bear in mind that actually the Lord is our ruler'? Certainly he begins to act more and more autocratically and to assume the trappings of royal power ('just one **ear-ring** of the **plunder**, please', *verse 24*), if not the name. And what are we to make of a man, one of whose sons is named Abimelech – 'my father is king'?

So to the account of the making of the ephod. Some suggest that the amount required to make this **ephod** (*verse 26*) indicates that some sort of representation of the Lord is intended here. Probably it is better to understand 'ephod' in its more normal sense (and to assume that either part of the wealth was used to make it or that the 'trappings' associated with it demanded the vast horde of **gold, ornaments, pendants and garments**). The ephod was, in fact, probably a priestly garment (probably modelled on that of the Aaronic priest) which contained some objects which were used to seek God's guidance. The sanctuary at Shiloh was the best part of a day's walk away and presumably Gideon (always prone to want special reassurance that he was in God's will) made the ephod with the intention of securing the guidance of God. Gideon had enjoyed the leading and the blessing of God. Perhaps his initial motives were good but he now was hankering after something which God had not ordained and, as Wilcock notes, 'guidance as man likes to receive it – can be nothing but a snare and a delusion'[39]. Thus the ephod became a **snare** (*verse 27*) and led (we surmise) Gideon and the people to view it selfishly and magically as a guarantee of the Lord's

---

39. Wilcock, p. 87.

blessing irrespective of their obedience and faithfulness. The writer of Judges, who does not always spell out the meaning of his tale (as we have seen), sums it up baldly: **'Israel prostituted themselves'** (*verse 27*).

How easily, too, our early aspirations to 'spend and be spent' for the Lord become exchanged for a comforting complacency arising from the fact that he is 'for' us. Such an attitude is nearer to the religion of Canaan than it is to true faith in the Lord. We need to be very watchful. If Gideon could fall, so can we.

The final verses of this chapter wind up the account of Gideon's life. Despite his failures the **land enjoyed peace for forty years** and the Midianite threat **did not raise its head again** (*verse 28*).

But all was far from well. The glory of God can be easily exchanged for personal glory (*8:28ff.*, especially *verses 29-31*). All that Gideon was resulted from the grace of God. But the very munificence of the Lord's grace ensnared him. Though he rejected the title of king he assumed all the trappings of an oriental monarch. His great confession, if such it was (*verse 23*), was belied by his actions. How easy it is for us to rejoice in our gifts and abilities and not in the giver and enabler. How readily we, too, exchange thoughts of the Lord's glory for that of our own. Again, the experience of Gideon should warn us.

Tragically his failures were sowing seeds for future disaster. He adopted the amoral life-style of ancient monarchs, and in terms reminiscent of ancient descriptions of kings we read that he **had seventy sons of his own, for he had many wives** (*verse 30*). If he lived like a king it is scarcely surprising that the following chapter describes a bitter dynastic battle. Anticipating a little, our author introduces us to Abimelech who certainly had royal ambitions (*verse 31*); but what on earth was Gideon doing having a concubine?

Small wonder, then, that disaster follows. Gideon had done much good (*verse 35*) but Klein, with justification, says, 'it is Gideon of all the judges who does most harm to Israel'[40]. His forgetfulness was followed by that of the nation (*verse 34*). During the remaining period of the judges they were never to know real peace again.

There are grounds for both warning and encouragement in the story of Gideon. May our victories be the equal of his, but may his failings never be those which ensnare us. May God help us!

Questions:

1. Gideon was faithful when cast upon the Lord but increasingly faithless when he didn't feel the need for God so much. What areas of your life are the ones in which you are most likely (according to these criteria) to let the Lord down? What can you do to avoid failure?

2. Our greatest failures are often seen when we do not demonstrate to others what we have received from God. How might this observation alert you to areas where you are vulnerable?

3. Spiritual gifts without spiritual grace are a great snare.

40. Klein, p. 68.

Illustrate this from the present chapter and reflect on how this might apply to areas of gifting that you have.

4. When is it right to be merciful and when should we be firm in judgement? How might you answer this question from the present chapter?

9:1-10:5: Abandoned to Choice

This is a passage that has perplexed many Christians. Not that the story is difficult to follow: many similar contemporary stories could be told. No! Rather the difficulty lies in the very fact that this is such a worldly story and it seems that the Lord has little or no part in it (being only mentioned in verses 23f. and 56f.). But this is, in fact, the whole point: here we are given a description of the people of God estranged from him. Or perhaps it would be more accurate to say that this chapter describes the consequences of God abandoning his people to the full consequences of the choices that they have made for themselves.

In fact the story has already begun by the time this chapter begins. The individualism of our modern society causes us to ignore both the testimony of the Bible and experience. We deceive ourselves into thinking that our failings are only our own. The reality is very different. What we are in private will inevitably affect what we are in public. And our failings and mistakes will invariably affect our dependants since few seem able to entirely shake off their heritage.

This lesson is vividly illustrated here. The last verses

of chapter 8 identified three of Gideon's failings. He adopted a kingly life-style (*verses 29-32*). He took up an immoral way of life (he engaged in multiple marriages, especially forbidden to rulers and married a Canaanite with whom he did not co-habit). Leviticus 18:18, Deuteronomy 17:17 and Genesis 2:24 suggest that he was wrong. And he was ensnared by false religious practices (*verses 22-27*). He may as **Jerub-Baal**, the Baal-fighter (*verse 1*), have effectively restrained Baalism. However, the consequences of his own failure in leadership made it almost inevitable that no sooner had Gideon died than **the Israelites prostituted themselves to the Baals** (*8:33*).

Immediately chapter 9 opens we are made aware of how Gideon's failings had severe consequences in the generation that followed him. First, because he had begun to adopt a kingly lifestyle his death issued in an attempt to establish a dynastic rule and that by means of methods which remain, even to this day, prevalent among the ungodly. Secondly, his immorality meant that there was little resistance to the adoption of immoral practices. The chapter is characterised throughout by thoroughly godless acts. Thirdly, the snare of the ephod had undermined the people's resistance to false religion. The moral and spiritual life of the people of God lay in ruins.

We may not be Gideons. But in our homes, workplaces and our fellowships we can have just as devastating an effect upon those around us. Our failure to adopt a consistent Christian lifestyle and to manifest the fruit of the Spirit can have a far greater and more damaging effect than we ever realise. We need to learn the lesson of this chapter well and pray for grace to be faithful.

Before we proceed further, we should notice that the Israelites worshipped **Baal Berith** (*verse 4*), the 'deity' at **Shechem** (*verse 2*) where there was a **great tree** and **pillar** and where Abimelech was recognised as king (*verse 6*). This was the very site where Joshua set up the pillar as a monument to remind the people of the Lord's covenant with them; a permanent reminder that the Lord was their king. It was also the place where the Tabernacle had been set up (Joshua 24:26). An added irony is the fact that Baal Berith means 'Baal of the covenant'. Since Shechem was also a city where Israelites, Canaanites and mixed-race peoples (such as Abimelech) lived together, the evidence points toward the cult of Baal Berith being a mixture of Baal worship and the veneration of the Lord. Here was a 'pick and mix' religion which the people had devised from what seemed the 'best bits' of the two faiths. It was a natural departure point from true worship for it did not involve outright rejection of the worship of God.

Thus the worship of Baal Berith provided a consumer-driven religion with God there to do his job as and when required. It was comfortably 'multi-faith'; lacking that claim to exclusivism which might lead to it being branded with intolerance. We can also see how Gideon's religious failures opened the door to the people moving in such a direction.

The last thing a worshipper of Baal Berith wants is one who contends against it! Those who are tolerant in religion are usually very intolerant of intolerance! Gideon had a nick-name, Jerub-Baal, which (as we have seen) means 'Baal fighter'. Small wonder then that Abimelech sought to destroy all those who might have tried to hold on to the old paths: **seventy of Jerub-Baal's sons** (*verse 2*). No surprise, either, that the project to eliminate them was funded **from the temple of Baal Berith** (*verse 4*).

With the clinching argument that **I am your flesh and blood** (*verse 2* and see *verse 3*), Abimelech succeeded in winning the full-support of the Shechemites. With temple money funding the local 'Mafia' thugs (*verse 4*) Gideon's family was soon eliminated **on one stone** (*verse 5*); surely a reference to a sacrifice to Baal made by means of human offerings. Are we intended to see a macabre echo of 6:25-27 here? Just as Gideon began his judgeship with an offering to the Lord, Abimelech, the anti-judge, sets out on his rule with a human sacrifice to Baal. The abandonment of the Lord's ways quickly leads to the adoption of worldly standards and increasingly depraved conduct. Modern Baal Beriths are no more able to stop such trends as the cult which flourished in Abimelech's time.

One of Gideon's sons, **Jotham**, escaped the carnage (*verse 5*). As a final act of defiance before he fled from Abimelech and passed from the pages of Scripture, he ascended the hill of **Gerizim** (*verse 7*). There, overlooking the city and making full use of the acoustics, he uttered a speech which culminated in a curse (*verses 8-20*).

There may be some significance in the fact that, according to Deuteronomy 27 and 28, Israel were to gather on the two hills of Ebal and Gerizim and proclaim from one to the other the blessings and the curses of God's covenant with them. Oddly, Gerizim was to be the hill from which the blessings were to be declared. Is this intended to be ironic? Did Jotham intend to convey the idea that God's blessings would become curses for the

69

Shechemites? Or did he imply that if the people learnt from his speech it would become a blessing to them? As so often in Judges we are left with tantalising questions. We cannot be sure.

Jotham began with a fable (*verses 8-15*) which is intended as a call to the people to act according to the light of truth and demonstrate the integrity that flows from such obedience (*verse 16*). This, he suggests, the people have failed to do (*verse 17*). With wisdom he recognises that if his verdict is correct (and he has little doubt that it is), then Abimelech and Shechem will 'self-destruct'.

At this point Jotham has grasped the fundamental nature of life which is out of step with the Lord. Sin, by its very nature, is divisive (as events in the Garden of Eden amply demonstrate). It has no cohesive power. Consequently, left to itself it destroys itself as its followers turn upon themselves. We shall have reason to refer to this again below.

Yet Jotham's speech seems flawed. Abimelech sought the throne of (at least part of) Israel. That is obvious enough. But we need also to notice that Jotham's fable does not revert to the view expressed by his father in 8:23: 'The LORD will rule over you'. He does not seem to criticise the fact that the people are seeking a king: only that they have asked the wrong person! In this respect, therefore, Abimelech and Jotham are no better than one another. They have forgotten the One who rules Israel.

So often this is true today, even among evangelicals. The 'rule of faith', the Bible, is often ignored. People do what they want. When churches come to make decisions it is seldom true that uppermost in the minds of all members is, 'What does the King want?' Far more often we come to press our own 'party' line, to selfishly press our views. Even our democratic voting systems can be a snare since we can find a way through without finding the will of the Lord. The Bible is no great advocate of democracy as the means of finding the Lord's will. Rather it advocates a spiritual sensitivity to the mind of Christ. He is King.

Israel were as a people dependent on their choice of leadership not the Lord's. Generally, throughout the Bible, leadership is 'charismatic': that is, it is the result of the gift of God, not the appointment of men. The judges had all been this sort of men and women. But Abimelech (and perhaps Jotham) sought to institutionalise the leadership of God's people. And the people were ready to make (and change) their choice rather than look for the one whom God would appoint.

The consequences were, of course, tragic. Since the leaders were appointed by the people they could be changed at their whim. The wrong leaders also adopted unspiritual methods to achieve their ends. They were appointed by those who were dominated by self-interest and unconcerned for the glory of God and they conducted themselves in the same way. Disaster and division speedily followed.

Again we need to notice how readily we fall into the same trap. Office in the church is to be manifested in service not self-advancement. Appointment is to be made not simply to 'fill up vacancies' or to ensure our 'party' is represented, but because God has equipped. Office is not to be jealously guarded. We are to be jealous only for the Lord. The tactics of the 'boardroom' have no place in the

71

Eldership or Diaconate or in any other place in the life of the Church. Departure from the Lord's pattern always leads to disaster: to petty squabbling and power struggles which strangle the life out of a church.

So we are unsurprised by the sequel for in the rest of the chapter we are introduced to a people who devour one another. Significantly a people who act in the way described here are not those to whom the Lord sends his Spirit but an **evil spirit** (*verse 23*). Thus, far from producing the fruit of the Spirit (Galatians 5:22ff.) and keeping in step with the Spirit they produced only the 'acts of the sinful nature' (Galatians 5:19-21). The result was, as it always is, mutual destruction. The people sought to overthrow the leader they had appointed and Abimelech sought to annihilate the very people over whom he ruled! In this way they experienced the wrath of God, the whiplash resulting from the perversion of God's way (*verses 56f.* and Romans 1:18-20).

It is strange to read that **God sent an evil spirit** (*verse 23*). But this reminds us that when Satan acts it is only with divine permission. However, there is more significance to the present reference than this. On the one hand it offers a contrast to 6:34 where the Spirit came upon Gideon so that he could save God's people. Here the evil spirit from God comes to punish. On the other hand, the evil spirit who appears at this point in fact only accelerates a process already taking place so as to shorten the period of self-destruction. Thus all this happened **after** a mere three years (*verse 22*). In a paradoxical way the sending of this evil spirit is an act of grace and mercy to the community of Israel!

The nature of the conflict is unsurprising. History is littered with examples of revolutionary movements being hijacked by the more radical members who then liquidate their former colleagues. Thus, if Abimelech the half-Israelite sought to give fresh impetus to the syncretic Baal Berith cult, **Gaal** reminded the Shechemites that their real religious roots lay further back in the full-blown paganism of a pure-bred Shechemite, **Hamor** (*verse 28*). He was obviously claiming pure-bred status for himself (*verse 29*)!

What is true politically is equally true spiritually. A Christian syncretism can only last for so long. Little by little, in the individual or society, the 'pagan' element in human nature reasserts itself. Sin breeds greater sin and eventually the total overthrow of any residual Christian influence and the restraint it provides takes place.

Thus, Jotham's prediction comes to pass. Gaal, double-crossed by **Zebul**, is overthrown (*verses 30-41*). 'Hopping mad' with Shechem, Abimelech vents his anger in the total destruction of Shechem (*verses 42-49*). In so doing he kills about a **thousand men and women** (*verse 49*) who had taken refuge in the **temple-tower of El-Berith** (*verse 46*). So much for the power of this god to save his people! Thus 'does Baal prove again his utter impotence to defend his people'[41].

Persistent sin darkens the ability of the mind to think! So Abimelech becomes a fool. Not content with the destruction of Shechem he turns on (innocent?) **Thebez** (*verse 50*), only to get stoned by a woman (*verse 52*). To be killed by a woman signified utter disgrace in the ancient world, hence Abimelech's response in verses 54 and

---

41. Jordan, p. 174.

55. Nevertheless, the woman administered the fatal blow. Moreover, as Jordan notes, 'stoning was the prescribed mode of capital punishment in the Old Testament'[42]; the means by which a person was declared spiritually a 'no-person'. Thus the career of the anti-judge or anti-king was brought to an end.

But if God has been scarcely mentioned in this chapter as men have gone their own way, this does not mean that he was not involved. With two words, **Thus God** (*verse 56*), the writer of the Book of Judges indicates that God has been at work to deliver Israel from itself. For this is surely the point of this chapter. No enemy attacks from without. Here the enemy is within and here, without any evidence that the people looked to him for help, the Lord uproots the core of evil from the very centre of the people's life. God emerges victorious with Baal destroyed by his own followers!

A final word from Jordan brings this sorry episode to an appropriate end: 'All this, however, blossomed from the seemingly minor compromises made by Gideon, the faithful warrior of God. Let each of us pray that we do not make similar compromises, for it is our children who will pay if we do.'[43]

But this is not the end of the story! This section of Judges ends with the mercy of God in raising up Tola and Jair (*10:1-5*). Significantly, nothing is mentioned about their mighty acts of conquest or of the enemy. Is it being over-speculative to suggest that this is because their work was quiet and unspectacular? Does it suggest that they 'rebuilt' Israel from within? This certainly seems very

42. Jordan, p. 175. 43. *Ibid.*, p. 176.

likely and was doubtless much needed after the ravages of Abimelech's short reign.

There may be hints that even these men were flawed; the size of **Jair**'s family (*10:4*) may suggest that he, perhaps, was modelling the exercise of his rule by pagan standards. However, large families were regarded as a blessing from God in Old Testament times (see, for example, Psalm 127:4,5) and the fact that Jair and his sons travelled on **donkeys** suggests that he was a man of peace. Certainly the Lord seems to have used both him, his sons and **Tola** to reassert his rule until (sadly) in 10:6 the people forgot him once again.

We may take great comfort from this. The Lord is always ready to help those who turn back to him. Sometimes, as here, he may even, apparently, take the initiative (though we must not presume upon him). Indeed, in another sense, it is only because he does this that we have any hope at all for, as Polzin says, 'in all fairness and honesty, Israel should not have survived'[44]! But hope there is for, in Bunyan's words, we have here an account of 'grace abounding to the chief of sinners'.

This passage challenges us to two great tasks: to live consistent Christian lives and to ensure that the Lord is King, above all, in our life and fellowship. To fail in either of these is to bring nothing but disaster upon us and those who follow us. May we find the grace to succeed.

---

44. R. Polzin, cited by Wilcock, p. 104.

Questions:

1. What evidence can you offer for the powerlessness of 'half-religion'? In what ways ought this affect the way you go about your own daily life?

2. Sin is self-destructive. Are the examples of this tendency that you can give from national and church affairs and your own life? What might you learn from this?

3. 'God sent an evil spirit'. Is your understanding of God big enough to be able to say this? If not, why not?

4. Trace the graciousness of God through this passage. What encouragement might you gain from this?

10:6-16: Love Triumphs Over Anger

With these verses we reach the half way point of the book. They also commence the last cycle of the stories of the judges which runs from 10:6-16:31. These 'saviours' were sent by God during a period of oppression from the Philistines (to the south and west) and the Ammonites (from the east). Two deliverers are described in detail: Jephthah (*10:17–12:7*) and Samson (*13:1–16:31*). Three are mentioned but briefly: Ibzan, Elon and Abdon (*12:8-15*). 10:6-16 sets the scene for all that is to follow.

With the exception of 2:6-3:6, the present verses describe, more fully than elsewhere, the cycle of sin-repentance-forgiveness-restoration which characterises the Book of Judges. But while, as Wilcock notes, we are 'back where we began – "the people of Israel did what was evil" (2:11), "the people of Israel again did what was evil" (10:6) – but we are now at a considerably lower level than we were then'[45]. The nation has abandoned itself fully to every alternative religion other than the true one (the 'complete' list of seven in verse 6 is surely intended to capture this thought!). Israel is **shattered and crushed** (*verse 8*) and **in great distress** (*verse 9*). Moreover, the Lord is **angry** (*verse 7*, 'the anger of the LORD burned' captures the force of the phrase better); angry enough to have **sold them** (*verse 7*) to his enemies. In addition to this, there is the question as to whether, this time, the Lord will step in and help them; **I will no longer save you**, he says in verse 13. In fact, therefore, it is less of a cycle and more of a spiral that is demonstrated in Judges.

The whole issue was not what the people professed but what they did. They may say, '**We have sinned against you, forsaking our God and serving the Baals**' (*verse 10*) but while this is as Wilcock notes 'a cry of recognition'[46], the sequel suggests that the Lord did not see this remorse as genuine repentance (*verses 11-16*).

Doubtless there were godly individuals in the nation. If Ruth and Boaz lived at the time of Gideon there would have been people like them during the lifetime of Jephthah. But the people as a whole were apostate and the people as a whole suffered.

Thus this passage emphasises that the community of God's people (which is clearly the focus here) can only know the favour of God as they live together as his servants. Indeed, the point can be made more strongly: only those who are servants of the Lord are his people.

---

45. Wilcock, p. 107.   46. *Ibid.*, p. 108.

We need to learn the same lessons. The Lord is concerned that each of us, individually, obey all that Jesus taught (Matthew 28:18-20). But our ambitions should not end with our own godliness. We should long for the godliness of all those who profess to be the people of God. Only when the church (and especially the local church) has together come to the point of common commitment to the Lord can we expect him to take away our reproach.

This passage is a graphic illustration of the fact that abandoning the true God makes no sense. We are first of all told the effects on the people from God's point of view (*verse 7*). The Lord became, as we have seen, angry and he sold them. Both these phrases emphasise that they were no longer his. Love had been replaced by wrath, personal possession by a complete transfer of rights to the enemies of God. There can be surely no more explicit picture of a people who, whatever their name, are no longer the people of God but citizens of the prince of this world. Too often today debates upon the nature of the church concentrate upon formal and outward characteristics. As a result a people can have all the formal marks of a church but, in fact, be a synagogue of Satan! We need then to give far more attention than we do to the questions raised here. Have we any right to call ourselves a church? Are we united in the service of the Lord? If we are, it will be seen in gracious lives and the enjoyment of the fruit of the Spirit. It will be seen in a devotion to Jesus which is evidenced in a delighted subservience to his will revealed in the Bible.

However, if losing fellowship with God is deemed an acceptable loss we need to note that this is not the only price to pay for abandoning him. Thus, the effects upon the people themselves are then described (*verses 8f.*). We are told that they were shattered, crushed, oppressed and distressed. They were hopeless and helpless. How vividly this describes so many churches (including many evangelical ones) today. How often its members fail to ask why they are in such a condition, being, perhaps, too bewildered to ask any sensible questions. And how frequently lives that have rejected God reproduce the same characteristics!

In this connection we need to notice that the suffering of the people was proportionate to their sin. Seven 'gods' had been embraced in place of the Lord (*verse 6*). Seven peoples oppressed the Israelites (*verse 11*). God never acts more harshly than we deserve. If we are in a sorry state it is not because the Lord is vindictive. Rather it represents the extent to which we have failed to live up to our calling to be servants. Looked at another way, the people's failure is emphasised by the fact that they had experienced seven mighty acts of salvation (*verses 11,12*) when previously in difficulty, but seemed incapable of learning the lesson.

It would be easy to conclude that verse 16 teaches that the Lord is ever ready to restore the truly repentant. Certainly the people took the sort of steps one would look for to demonstrate genuine repentance; **they got rid of the foreign gods among them and served the Lord**. The people showed a true sorrow which was evidenced in a total renunciation of those idols which had ensnared them. When they acted in this way they found that the Lord simply **could bear Israel's misery no longer**.

But, as Davis notes, verse 16b does not link the Lord's response to their 'repentance but to her misery or suffering'. So he adds, 'Our hope does not rest in the sincerity of our repentance but in the intensity of Yahweh's compassion.'[47]

This is, at one and the same time, both a warning and an encouragement. We cannot presume upon God's mercy time and again. Repentance (however genuine) does not itself lay claim upon God so that he must turn and favour us again. We cannot presume upon him in this way.

And yet, even though our failure may be great and our penitence imperfect, we can still hope in his compassion; for love overcomes wrath. It was this love that sent the Son of God to Calvary to bear the punishment that was, by rights, ours.

As with so much in the Book of Judges this is a solemn passage. Yet it also sets before us God's grace and mercy in the tenderest terms. What encouragement to us to become the people we are called to be, 'servants of the most High'.

Questions:

1. What evidence can you offer for the fact that turning away from God to other 'more attractive' things rarely brings anything but heartache?

2. How might the teaching about penitence and grace apply to your life or your church's life?

---

47. Davis, p. 136.

10:17-12:15: Salvation by Nobody

10:6-16 concluded with the reader on tiptoe. How will the Lord show that **he could bear Israel's misery no longer** (*verse 16*). These chapters describe how the Lord raised up **Jephthah** (and his successors **Ibzan, Elon** and **Abdon**) to restore the people.

The Lord's compassion seems to have outworked itself in his galvanising the people to action. For eighteen years the Israelites had passively accepted their situation, presumably appealing to their helplessness in the face of their enemies. But now a spirit of resistance is in the air! Gathered at **Mizpah** (*10:17*) they decide that action is required (*verse 18*). The people of God are always, of course, helpless to improve their situation if the Lord is not with them. Yet this is no excuse for inactivity. Thus, newly awakened to the fact that God is not honoured by their situation and its reproach, they 'get moving'.

There is something unspiritual about our unwillingness to plan ahead as the Lord's people. Of course, we are utterly dependent on him and he can always act in an unexpected and unplanned way (as he had with Gideon). But looking to him we are expected to give thought and planning in attempting to undertake his work.

But who were the people to ask to lead them? There was, in fact, only one candidate who was obviously equipped for the task: Jephthah. Like David later he had had to learn to fend for himself without the support of family and clan (*11:1-3*). He was probably a mercenary soldier of some sort; **a mighty warrior** (*verse 1*). He clearly had gifts of leadership for others gathered round him (*verse 3*). However, he was illegitimate; the son of a

prostitute (*verse 1*). **His father was Gilead** suggests that 'any man in the region could have been his father'[48] and the fact that his mother was a prostitute may suggest that she was not an Israelite (since prostitution was forbidden). 'Born and bred' Gileadites (*verse 2*, **wife** here probably represents 'wives of the tribe') had, therefore, expelled him from the tribe lest they lose out by his taking a share in the tribal lands.

Paradoxically, this experience of trial seems (as with so many) to have been the making of him. When he appears in the story he is already a skilled diplomat and soldier. He was also a godly man (*11:9, 30f.*) who knew the dealings of God with his people in the past very well (*11:13ff.*).

Thus, the people who had rejected him in the past when they were more occupied with their selfish interests had to 'eat humble pie' before Jephthah in asking him to lead them (*11:4-6*) and he was understandably careful before accepting their invitation (*11:7-11*). He was also anxious to point out that if victory over the Ammonites followed it would be because **the LORD gives them to me** (*verse 9*).

But can God be in all this diplomacy? The answer is a resounding 'Yes' as verse 11 shows for, as Wilcock notes, the words **he repeated all his words before the LORD in Mizpah** are 'no mere formality'[49]. Once the Lord had been moved to compassion, the deliberations, plans, strategies and diplomacies that the people took were seen to be ordered by him to achieve his purposes of salvation.

There is comfort in knowing that the Lord can use such disadvantaged people as Jephthah even though this is not

---

48. Jordan, p. 193. 49. Wilcock, p. 111.

the most important lesson of the story. Nor is the fact that he was, like Jesus after him, 'a man of sorrows and acquainted with grief'. Rather, the lesson we are to learn is that when we return to the Lord it is often those whose leadership we have rejected that we must return to. Above all, we are to place ourselves, once more, under the authority of God and his will.

This passage is sanguine, however, about the harsh realities in leading the reformation of God's people. Jephthah found four steps necessary to bring about their restoration.

First of all, he began with diplomacy (*11:12-28*). But he was no mere politician. What he set forth was the will of the Lord. He urged the Lord's enemies to be subject to his will. Several commentators note that his argument is carefully crafted. Having established the basis for the Ammonite hostilities (*verses 12-13*) he replied first of all by an appeal to history (*verses 15-22*). Israel had not (as claimed) taken Ammonite territory. The land north of the Arnon had been Amorite when Israel entered Canaan and had been won from Sihon, the Amorite. Moreover, Sihon's territory had been given to Israel by the Lord (*verse 21*). This reads like a gentle but firm threat; if the Lord has done this once he can do it again, especially to usurpers!

The second part of the argument is an appeal to theology (*verses 23-24*). It is possible but unlikely that Jephthah believed in the reality of non-Israelite gods. The force of his argument is rather, 'The Lord has given us our land to live in. Rest content with the territory your "gods" have apportioned to you.'

The third stage of his argument is an appeal to precedent

(*verse 25*). If in fact there is no legitimate claim to the territory in question and the true reason for Ammonite aggression is hatred of Israel then, suggests Jephthah, why not follow the precedent of Balak who had stopped short of outright warfare.

Finally, Jephthah offers an argument from silence (*verse 26*). If there was a genuine grievance, how was it that nothing had been mentioned about it during the previous three hundred years?

Sadly, the king of Ammon paid no attention (*verse 28*) and, since his diplomacy had failed, Jephthah found it necessary to wage outright war against those who had proved intransigent. Empowered by **the Spirit of the Lord** (*verse 29*), **the Lord gave** the Ammonites **into his hands** (*verse 32*). Eighteen years of misery were wiped out in one short military action when the Lord was on the side of his people!

Before we pick up verses 30, 31 and 34-40, we need to note one other incident associated with this military campaign. Jephthah found (as so many have done since) that the greatest enemy when undertaking the Lord's work is often the enemy within (*12:1-6*).

We have already encountered the Ephraimites (*8:1-3*). They liked to think that they were the leading tribe. They resented anyone else usurping the position that they believed was rightfully theirs. In Gideon's day they had, nevertheless, fought on the side of the people of God. However, their pride had apparently grown ever greater in the meanwhile and they refused to support Jephthah. Thus he says, **although I called, you didn't save me ... you wouldn't help** (*12:2, 3*). In fact they had already crossed the Jordan from their tribal territory east of the river (as the sequel shows) and had **come up to fight** (*verse 3*). If they couldn't have the dignity they thought they deserved they intended to do all that they could to bring down 'the Lord's anointed'. Hence the trumped up charges which manifestly didn't ring true (*verse 1*); they didn't need them, since any excuse would do!

All this explains Jephthah's very different response from that of Gideon. The Ephraimites, by their rebellion, had effectively declared themselves to be the enemies of the Lord. They could no longer be tolerated. No longer the Lord's people they had to be exterminated just like the Canaanites before them. Numbers 26:37 tells us that Ephraim numbered 32,500 men when Canaan was entered. The present event took place no more than 300 years later. Thus, to lose **42,000** (*verse 6*) must have been a virtual 'wipe-out'. The power of Ephraim was destroyed for generations to come.

How often have those who have sought to restore the Lord's people encountered the same difficulties. They have proclaimed the Lord's will, they have had to fight against the power that the ungodly have gained over the church. But they have found that the greatest enemy is the enemy within, those who like to think of themselves as the people of God but who show by their conduct that they know nothing of genuine spiritual life. Sadly when such radical action is required we often have cold feet. But there is a time when we must act for the glory of God and the unity of his people, when we can no longer tolerate ungodliness in the midst of the people of God.

Sadder still is the fact that we can see that the overall

decline during the period of the judges is such that the people are beginning to speak differently and to act independently, to the ultimate destruction of the people of God (or, at least, a substantial portion of them). Unity lived out in obedience to God's will and under the leadership that he gives is alone able to stem this self-destructive urge.

The story of Jephthah is difficult to interpret. But nowhere is this more so than in the final incident (*11:30, 31, 34-40*) and many good Christians are divided over whether a human sacrifice takes place here. On balance, this seems unlikely. The reasons are the following:

1) Jephthah's vow clearly had in mind another human being. The phrase **whatever comes out of my house** (*verse 31*) is best translated by 'whoever' and he is, therefore, not likely to have had a family pet or some other animal in view. But human sacrifice was never practised in Israel and was strictly forbidden in the Law with which Jephthah shows considerable familiarity. Jephthah must have acted entirely out of character to have a human sacrifice in mind.

2) The whole emphasis upon the mourning of his daughter is upon her perpetual virginity ('**I will never marry**') not her premature death (*verses 37, 38, 39*). This is strange if she was to be offered up as a human sacrifice.

3) There is no need to interpret **burnt offering** (*verse 31*) literally. It is quite possible that it had a metaphorical usage and referred to something wholly devoted to the Lord. Since there were under the Old Covenant women such as

Anna who devoted themselves to service in or around the Tabernacle and Temple (and, in Anna's case, seem to have forgone marriage or re-marriage), it seems likely that Jephthah's daughter may well have been devoted to the Lord in this way.

4) While recognising that biblical narrative does not always make its judgements clear upon events that are described, the story would surely have contained some veiled criticism of Jephthah had he so blatantly acted against the Law of God. Moreover, it is difficult to understand how the Lord could use such a person as the deliverer of his people; although he is a God of amazing grace!

Thus (though many offer other conclusions), it would seem most likely that Jephthah made a foolish vow in which he pledged the first person who came from his home to the service of the Lord. He must have known the risk he took that it might be his daughter. Perhaps he thought this might increase the 'power' of the vow. His grief is understood when we realise that since she was his only child he thereby removed the possibility that his name would live on in Israel. This was the ambition of every Israelite man, especially one who was the 'son of none'. Sadly, Jephthah was eventually buried **in a town in Gilead**, an anonymous place with no family connections (*12:7*).

The folly of the vow was compounded by the fact that it indicated that Jephthah had unworthy views of the Lord. He is a God of grace who is not manipulated (as Jephthah sought to do) by the vows of men. Vows are to be a response to grace not a means to achieve it.

Yet despite his foolishness, he was not willing to break his vow (*verse 35*) and his daughter was willing to submit (*verse 36*). Though we might consider that there were grounds for evading the implementation of his vow, he went through with it. He was resolved to go through with what he had promised. His was a dedicated if misguided faith which challenges us still!

So Jephthah was a hero of the faith (Hebrews 11:32) – but a flawed hero. Yet of all the judges he was perhaps the greatest for he did not fall to the depths that either Gideon or Samson did. Considerable comfort lies here. We all have our faults and our unworthy views of God. Yet he does not reject us as flawed vessels or 'seconds'. Whether our tasks are great or menial he will readily use us if, with all our limitations, we seek his honour.

Once again we are given cause to marvel that in this solemn book there are such testimonies to the love and mercy of God to men and women similar to us. May this mercy and love stir us up to faithfully put into practice the more difficult aspects of its message!

Finally, this section of Judges concludes with brief references to three other 'minor' judges; **Ibzan** (*12:8-10*), **Elon** (*12:11*) and **Abdon** (*12:13-15*). Little of significance is said about these men. However, after Jephthah who led Israel for six years (*12:7*), a further period of twenty-five years of peace followed.

In addition, the verses clearly imply that Ibzan was an older man with a large family. These things are invariably regarded as a blessing from God in the Old Testament and indicative of such an absence of strife as enabled children to mature, to be married and grow old. We are also told that Ibzan carefully married his children in such a way as to establish a web of relationships with other clans in Israel. This suggests that his particular contribution to Israel was to seek to ensure that the fragmentation of the nation (reflected in the previous paragraph) was overcome.

We cannot be sure about his success. Some commentators note that there is no reference to there being 'peace' during the periods that these three men ruled. There may have been no enemies without, but (it is suggested) there was no real peace within the nation.

Abdon is described in terms which suggest similar conclusions to those we have offered for Ibzan. However, there is one ominous note. He came from and was buried in an area of the land sufficiently dominated by the **Amalekites** as to be described as their **hill country** (12:15). This reminds us that Israel was far from realising its true calling and it prepares us for the events of Samson's life which follow; where we shall discover Israel helpless even in the midst of that territory it might have thought it could reasonably secure as its own.

Questions:

1. Consider the disadvantages that Jephthah encountered in his early life and the problems he had to face in later life as a result. What can we learn from the way that he faced these things and what comfort can we draw from the fact that God used him?

2. 'Just leave it to God'. What place should planning and

action occupy when we want to see the Lord at work among us? Reflect upon the lessons which this passage gives.

3. Jephthah went through with a foolish promise he made to the Lord. What sensible promises have you made and have you faithfully followed them through? If not, why not?

4. In what practical ways might you seek to work for unity and peace within the people of God?

5. In what way can we today help destroy the work of God? What are the lessons we ought to learn from this passage?

6. What are the distinctive characteristics of the various judges whom we have encountered so far? What do they teach us about the people that God uses and what do they reveal about God himself?

13:1-25: A Surprising Beginning

The detailed account of the announcement of Samson's birth in this chapter which precedes the all so familiar stories of Samson's life (chapters 14-16) emphasises that his life-story is clearly intended as the climax of the Book of Judges. Moreover, his judgeship is dealt with in more considerable detail than the dozen who preceded him. Samson is thus depicted, in all his uniqueness and failings, as a judge *par excellence*. We shall find this fact significant in the interpretation of his life.

There are two important matters of background which help us to understand these stories. The first is historical. Though the historical background is not easy to reconstruct the following seems the most likely. At the time that Jephthah was raised up to defeat the immediate danger posed by the enemies from the east, the Lord also raised up Samson to begin to deal with the longer-term and more dangerous threat from the south and west (*verse 5*). The Philistines were a maritime people (possibly from Crete) who had established themselves on the coastal plain of Palestine. They were merchant seamen. However, gradually they sought to extend their influence inland. Initially this seems to have been achieved through intermarriage and trade (this would explain why the people of Judah did not see them as enemies, 15:9ff.). Shamgar had been raised by the Lord to alert the people of Israel to the danger (*3:31*), but his example was soon forgotten. Israel was in danger of being eliminated as a distinct people without anyone appearing to notice what was happening! This menace had to be dealt with. Thus over a period of 40 years, first Samson and then Samuel were used to break the threat of the Philistines before David finally conquered them (see 1 Samuel 7 and 2 Samuel 5:17-25). While Samson lived Eli was probably High Priest. The battle of Aphek (1 Samuel 4:1-11), in which the ark was taken, could well have followed the events in chapter 16 and been a reprisal raid for the damage wrought by Samson in his death.

But the theological context is still more important. In the beginning of the Old Testament story, the Creation and the Fall were followed by the promise of a Deliverer

91

in Genesis 3:15. This promise was then located within the descendants of Abraham, Isaac and Jacob (Genesis 12:1-3 and parallels). Paradise regained by the hands of a Deliverer was promised. By the time of the Book of Judges the people are in a land which God had promised to them in terms which were paradisaical, 'the land of milk and honey'. But repeated failure through the weakness of the flesh (a weakness found even in some, if not all, their judges) has left the people no nearer the realisation of God's promise than at the beginning of the Book, 300 years earlier. The time has come for the people to look to the Lord to raise up his Deliverer. And at this point the unique preparation of Samson is described (*13:1-25*). Is he, then, the promised seed who will break the serpent's head, one through whom paradise will be restored and the nations blessed, one who will in himself set the example for the people to follow?

But we run beyond ourselves! The story begins with a familiar ring. Once again **the Israelites did evil in the eyes of the LORD** and were **delivered into the hands of** their enemies; this time **the Philistines** (*verse 1*). In view of the fact that the periods of judgement have tended to increase during the Book we are, perhaps, not surprised to learn that this time **forty years** elapsed.

However, several surprises do follow! First of all, we are not told that the Israelites cried out to the Lord in their distress. Davis says: 'They have, apparently, become accustomed to servitude; in fact ... they are content with it, are surprised should anyone suggest otherwise (see *15:11*).'[50]

---

50. Davis, p. 160.

Secondly, though an announcement of salvation follows (*verse 5*), the story-cycle of Judges is interrupted by our being introduced to a childless couple from the small group of Danites (here called a clan to emphasise their fewness) left behind when the majority of the tribe migrated northwards (as described in chapters 17 and 18 but which had already occurred, probably during the time of Gideon). The apparent insignificance of the family is stressed by the fact that only the husband's name is recorded!

However, little by little (and with consummate artistry) the author tells his story until we are 'on tiptoe' at the end of the chapter; aware that from the most unlikely beginnings a remarkable act of salvation is about to unfold.

Thus, we are told (in a story which echoes the births of the great patriarchs Isaac and Jacob) that a **sterile** woman is **going to conceive and have a son** (*verse 3*). Moreover, this son (and even his mum!) is to be a **Nazirite** from birth (*verses 4, 5*); a fact which is so important that it is repeated several times for emphasis (see *7, 13, 14*). The Nazirite is fully described in Numbers 6. The Nazirite vow was voluntary and temporary. Not so with Samson. His was to be a life wholly dedicated to God: a life which would set before the people the calling of all God's people to be devoted to the Lord. By obedience to God and dependence on him Samson was, also, to show that by faith the people might call upon supernatural resources to deliver them from all their enemies. This is important. In the sequel Samson's great strength was not magically produced by his long hair. It was in faithfully obeying his vow (symbolised by the uncut hair) that he triumphed in God (as Hebrews 11:32 recognises). Thus set apart, the

93

child will **begin the deliverance of Israel** (*verse 5*).

The fact that **the angel of the LORD** (*verse 3*) reappears to make this announcement (compare *6:11*) only goes to build up the sense of expectation which reaches fever-pitch when we are told that **the Spirit of the LORD began to stir** the child when he had grown up (*verse 25*). Thus **Samson** is introduced to us (*verse 24*).

In the meanwhile we are introduced to the hesitant steps to faith of Manoah, the robust trust of his wife, and the strange incident in which the angel of the LORD 'goes up in smoke', in the flame arising from the burnt offering. The **burnt offering** (*verse 16*) was the offering made to remove sin (see Leviticus 1:4). Thus the angel of the LORD who, as Manoah recognises, is none other than the Lord himself (*verse 22*), ascends in the very flame.

All this suggests that this chapter is intended to show us that God appears and takes his own gracious initiative to deliver his sinful, undeserving people. Perhaps the last paragraph hints at the cost that God himself expends in saving them; a fact which may give this story typological significance (i.e., it offers a picture of the more wonderful sacrifice of the Son of God for the sins of the world which is revealed in the New Testament).

Moreover, the sequel does, of course, present Samson to us as a 'tarnished hero'[51]. In the context of the Book of Judges this causes the author to long for a king (*17:6; 18:1; 19:1; 21:25*). But at length the failure of the monarchy will lead the Old Testament writers to look for the Great King and Judge who, alone, will be able to accomplish all the purposes of God – the Lord Jesus Christ. Thus,

51. Lewis, p. 72.

1) Among all men, sacred history shows that the promises of God can have no other fulfilment than in Jesus.

2) The passage also points us to Jesus as the One who sets before us the standard of devotion to God which is to characterise all of us. Just as Samson was intended to set a challenge and example to the people (and, in part, failed), so the Lord Jesus sets a perfect example to us.

3) The passage teaches us that by faith we can and ought to be more than conquerors. The resources of the Holy Spirit which enabled Samson to undertake supernatural feats is the same Spirit who dwells within us to empower us to spiritual victory.

4) Further, we are reminded that all of us are debtors to grace. Samson's birth was a remarkable initiative by the Lord which was undertaken for the helpless. So is our spiritual birth. By grace when spiritually dead we were 'born again'.

5) Finally, the circumstances of Samson's ministry remind us that the greatest danger to the people of God (both individually and collectively) is not the outright threat but the insidious and gradual encroachment of the enemy. We need to be ever watchful.

Questions:

1. As you reflect upon your own testimony, how does this chapter highlight the way in which God's grace has been demonstrated in your life?

2. What encouragement can you gain personally and as a member of your local church, by the fact that Samson's great work began with an insignificant family from a small clan in a remote village?

3. In what ways today do you think that individuals and the church can insidiously slip into a situation where they/it are blind to the need of repentance?

4. Reflect upon the different ways in which Manoah and his wife responded to the Angel of the LORD's appearance and message. What might you learn from this?

14:1-16:31: Faith Gone Astray

Chapter 13 has prepared us for viewing the judgeship of Samson as the climax of the Book of Judges. God proves faithful to his Word in what follows (compare *13:5* with *16:27-30*). Yet, as we shall see, the life of Samson is one of a man of faith gone tragically astray. As such he highlights the weakness of the judges as a whole and points to the need for a king (*17:6; 18:1; 19:1; 21:25*) and, beyond that, directs us to the Incarnation of Jesus as the answer to mankind's needs and the fulfilment of God's promises.

All this becomes very quickly apparent. Samson,

despite the uniqueness of his preparation, appears as the weakest judge of all, for, as Klein reminds us, 'physical passion [is] the lowest kind of subjugation'[52].

Thus, wandering in nearby **Timnah** (about four miles from 'home') he sees a young girl who is, as we say, 'a cracker'. This is the force of the Hebrew in 14:2 when it says, '**I have seen a Philistine *woman*'**. This is the first example in the life of Samson of what might be called his 'living above the law'. History records time and again the stories of men and women who believed that they were too great or important to be hedged in by the normal standards of morality. This seemed to be a weakness with Samson. It is true that the only marriages expressly forbidden in Exodus 34:16 and Deuteronomy 7:3, 4 were with Canaanitish women. But the reasons assigned for this prohibition were equally applicable to marriages with daughters of the Philistines. The grief of his parents (*14:3*) and the absence of family at the wedding seems to emphasise that he was breaking the traditions of Israel. The fact that, in 14:1-3, the woman is identified as a **Philistine** on three separate occasions seems to emphasise this.

Similarly, his treatment of his parents went against the very fundamental principles of family life which the Lord had revealed (Exodus 20:12).

Certainly, Samson seemed to have lost sight of the fact that the Lord is a holy God who expects holiness of his people. Time and again he ignored the demands of his Nazirite vow. We can scarcely imagine he did not drink wine at his own wedding party (*14:10*) and on several

---

52. Klein, p. 118.

occasions he was in contact with corpses. Perhaps the latter was excluded from his vow because of his calling to be a judge but his general laxness is obvious.

The story of Samson is characterised by the repetition of the phrase **did not know**. It occurs for the first time in 14:4; his parents did not know. Time and again the author of Judges uses this phrase to ironically hint that more is taking place in the unfolding story than was perceived at the time by those involved. This is the case here. Manoah and his wife were the only people (apart from Samson, if they had shared it with him) who were aware of his destiny. Yet his first recorded adult act was to flaunt the will of the One who had destined him to be judge.

But what they did not know was that **this was from the LORD** (*verse 4*); for the paradox is that God sometimes accomplishes his will through the unwitting and undeserving. As the poet William Cowper once observed, 'God moves in a mysterious way, his wonders to perform'.

There is much that is mysterious about verses 5–9. What was Samson (the Nazirite, of all people!) doing in a vineyard? And did he not refrain from telling his parents where he had found the honey (*verse 9*) because he knew that they would be grieved (and his mother's Nazirite status compromised) by the fact that he had touched a corpse? Further, how strange that it was there that the **Spirit of the LORD came upon him in power** so that in tearing the lion apart he discovered (for the first time?) God's gift to him of great strength.

It is not always easy to understand God's ways! But what we can learn here is that God often involves himself in very 'messy' situations, weaving his purposes into flawed lives and their paradoxical circumstances. While this is not a basis for failing to seek his glory above everything else, it is a comfort to those who have fallen and a reassurance that the messiest situation is not such that he cannot fulfil his purposes in and through it.

So Samson **tore the lion apart with his bare hands** (*14:6*). He is often, of course, depicted as a giant among men: a man bursting with brute strength. This picture is almost certainly wrong. The Old Testament never fails to dwell upon physical peculiarities. Saul and Goliath offer two obvious examples. But no mention is made of Samson's physique: on the contrary men are intrigued as to where his strength comes from (*16:6ff.*). This is not the sort of question asked of a giant for the answer is all too obvious.

In fact, of course, the story is quite explicit that the strength was not naturally possessed by Samson. His strength is repeatedly traced to the working of the Holy Spirit (*14:6, 19; 15:14*) and the departure of the Lord rendered him as powerless as any other man (*16:21*). Samson himself recognised his dependence on the Lord (*15:18; 16:28*). Thus, the writer to the Hebrews recognised that Samson's victories and exploits were those of a man of faith (Hebrews 11:32).

As such, Samson was a living example of what the people of God might do by faith. He remains a vivid illustration of what we, ourselves, may do by dependence on the Lord. He was engaged in spiritual warfare (a fact which is clearly set forth in the final episode in Dagon's temple) and, by faith, was able to ransack the powers of darkness. As the people of God the same resources are ours to undertake the impossible, by faith (Ephesians 3:20f.). Paul's words apply 'through all generations' after all!

A 'macho' man in the ancient world was expected to have wit as well as strength. So, at the wedding feast, Samson comes out with a **riddle** (based on his experience with the lion) which confounds the Philistine guests and, after four days of 'lubrication' by drink, makes them angry (*14:15*). Under pressure from the Philistines, his wife is able to wheedle the reply from him (with a typical 'woman's guile'?). The Philistines win the day (*14:18a*).

Or do they? Samson is not slow to spot the 'interference' with his wife (which he interprets in semi-sexual terms; they had **ploughed** with his **heifer**). Aroused to anger his previous friendship with the Philistines is turned to rage. **The Spirit of the LORD came upon him in power** and he gets his thirty suits! **Burning with anger** toward the Philistines he stomps off home (*14:19*). Samson was to begin the deliverance of Israel from the hands of the Philistines (*13:5*) – the beginning of the beginning has taken place.

Samson is the sort of person whose anger burns hot and cold. Several months pass; but when the time of year comes when thoughts once again turn to love, Samson decides to return to his wife and begin fathering a family (the gift of a **young goat** in the ancient world seems to have carried this 'implication').

But here we are introduced to the fact that Samson 'did not know' something! Assuming that Samson had gone 'never to return', his wife's father had given her in marriage to the best man (*14:20*). Despite a reasonable offer (there is no reason to believe the **younger sister** was not actually

more attractive), Samson's acute sense of personal injustice is aroused against the Philistines once more. And when Samson gets angry, he 'gets even' (*15:3-5*)!

The Philistines then fuel the fire of his anger by exercising gruesome retribution on his wife's family (*15:6*). Samson's response was predictably swift (*15:7, 8*).

By this time Samson has become more than a minor irritant to the Philistines, especially as they are the ruling power in the region. So off they go to the town nearest to **Etam**, his current home, and demand that he is given over to them as a prisoner (*15:9-10*). At this point we are introduced to a sobering fact; the Israelites have become so accustomed to their subjugation to the Philistines that Samson is an irritation to them too!

What more clear-cut evidence could the people of God have had that the Lord planned to deliver them than the early exploits of Samson (*14:19-15:7*)? But look what happened! They pointed out to Samson that they were powerless in the hands of the Lord's enemies and reproached him for disturbing the status quo; **What have you done to us?** (*15:11*)! At length they would have no choice but to receive him as their judge (*15:20*) and they would honour him in his death (*16:31*), but their initial failure to respond to the Lord's man was a pathetic show of unbelief.

How easy it is for us to glory in our reproach, to turn faithlessly away from those whom God has raised up for our salvation. How easily we prefer the quiet life of defeat to the exciting but demanding life of faith. Yet God gives us enough evidence (and his Word ought to be enough) that he has called us to victory.

Of course, Samson's success did not come overnight or without setbacks. He had to undertake many of his exploits alone. Yet the man who began by wreaking havoc in Timnah (a village only four miles away from his home in Zorah) ended up such a scourge to the great cities of the Philistines that the leaders went to considerable expense to have him removed from the scene (*16:5*) and had a national day of celebration in the capital Gaza when he was finally neutralised (as they thought!). There is no reason that we cannot begin by faith in 'our small corner' just as Samson did and do 'exploits' for the Lord.

The pathetic argument, 'No, we won't kill you. We just want you to go as a prisoner to the Philistines' (*15:12,13*), only serves to emphasise the need for the Israelites to be delivered from their own apathy to their tragic condition. But the Lord will not tolerate it! Thus, **the Spirit of the Lord came upon him in power** and Samson effected such a strike against a **thousand** of the Philistines (*15:14,15*) that he was established for **twenty years** as leader of Israel and the Philistines became subject to Israel (this would explain why he could freely walk about in **Gaza**, one of the major Philistine towns, *16:1*).

Yet this was all of the Lord (as *15:18,19* demonstrate). The **great victory** was **given** by the Lord, as Samson himself recognised. He was still human, he got thirsty and was dependent on the Lord even for a drink of water! For Israel, and for us, the lesson ought to have been obvious!

We cannot, however, read the story of Samson without a profound sense of sadness as tragedy unfolds. Several weaknesses, in addition to those we have already noticed, are to be found (and increasingly appear) in Samson.

Samson treated the grace of God too lightly. It is a fact all too often displayed in the lives of professing Christians that they presume upon the grace of God. 'God must favour us,' we suggest, 'for it is his character to have mercy.' This failing is illustrated on several occasions in the life of Samson. Perhaps the best example of this is the way he treats Delilah's questions as a great joke (*16:6-16*). Divine gifts were being treated lightly. How readily we can do the same. Yet, again like Samson, how readily we presume we can draw upon such divine resources when we want them.

Verses 1-5 of chapter 16, however, make the same point. Samson's wife may have been a Philistine but she was not (so far as we know) a prostitute. Here, however, Samson engages a **prostitute**. The whole city would have known Samson, so it is not surprising that the Philistines were aware of his presence and location and **lay in wait for him all night at the city gate**. Quite apart from the fact that his witness to pagans would have been compromised by such conduct, he only escapes by a misuse of his God-given power.

The feat recorded here is phenomenal. That **he took hold of the doors of the city gate, together with the two posts, and tore them loose, bar and all** was superhuman in itself. But to carry those posts, presumably over several days, uphill to **Hebron**, nearly 40 miles away, is utterly amazing! Yet this bravado exercised in escaping from a prostitute's bed was a dreadful misuse of a God-given gift.

Perhaps the writer of the Book of Judges saw this as a parable of Israel's own experience; had they not experienced many awe-inspiring acts of God's salvation? But had they not also come to take for granted his grace?

The latter portion of this chapter describes this great but flawed man trapped by his own sinful nature. We have no reason to doubt that the greater part of the (unrecorded) twenty years of Samson's judgeship were marked by his faithfulness. Nevertheless, the warning signs of the weakness which eventually destroyed him were there from the start. Sensuality led to his desire for a wife among the Philistines rather than among his own people. Later that unbridled weakness led to a liaison with a prostitute (from which dangerous situation he escaped only by a misuse of his God-given strength) and, finally, the taking of a mistress in **Delilah**. This last relationship was his ruin. Perhaps he had even traded on the mercy of God in past failures in seeking a fresh relationship with her. However, at length the wrath of a holy God must catch up even with those who are his sinning children.

This is, perhaps, emphasised by what appears to be a deliberate play on words in this section. The name Samson is closely related to the Hebrew word for 'sun'. Delilah is related to 'night'. Ensnared by 'night' Samson ends up blind and unable to see the sun. What an irony! Darkness has overcome light because of Samson's moral failures.

16:20 must be one of the saddest verses in the Bible. Heedless of his failings and presumptuous of God's grace Samson eventually reached the point where, unknown to him, the Lord had deserted him. Samson must have realised when he woke up that his hair had gone. However, he had sailed close to the wind with so many of the other Nazirite vows and the Lord had stayed with him. How was he to know that this time **the LORD had left him**? Yet with such grace gone there were no resources left to encounter the enemy and Samson – the Saviour of the Lord's people – ended up the butt of the jokes of the ungodly. He was required to **perform for them** (*16:25*), like a performing bear at a circus.

More seriously still, the Philistines thought that they had conquered him who is the Lord of hosts: pointedly celebrating Samson's capture in the Temple of Dagon and praising **our god who has delivered our enemy into our hands** (*16:24*); words that should have been on the lips of the Israelites!

This is the tragic sequel of unrepented sin and disobedient presumption upon the grace of God. The Lord would sooner suffer reproach than his people's sin. He must punish his children in love (Amos 3:2). And, as the writer of Judges believed, Samson was but a parable of the people as a whole.

How close do we sail to the wind? How sure can we be that our powerlessness has a different cause than the one set before us in the story of Samson?

Yet time and again in these studies in Judges the last word has been mercy: and so it is here. Tragedy at least brought Samson to his senses. As **the hair on his head began to grow again** (*16:22*) so, it appears, he was brought to repentance and renewed faith. This is demonstrated in his final prayer (*16:28-30*). Thus, in his death, he fulfilled the promise of 13:5, by destroying the entire leadership of the Philistine nation (*16:23, 27*); **three thousand** in one 'fell swoop'.

But Samson could never escape the consequences of his folly. He was still blind and his final and greatest victory was (like Nelson at Trafalgar) also the means of his death. The Lord does forgive. But often we must bear the burden of past folly around with us. Samson ended his life having achieved all that the Lord had promised. But surely there was a better way than the one he took. How poignant, therefore, is verse 31: the final word on a man who had achieved so much but...

Thus, the final episode of Samson's life faces us with two concluding lessons. The Lord is merciful. But how much better to be faithful to him and to escape such tragedy!

Questions:

1. Can you think of any areas in your life where you are tempted to presume upon God's grace and live 'beyond' the law? What warnings does this passage offer to those of us who persist in such a lifestyle?

2. 'God moves in a mysterious way'; how does this passage teach this truth and what might we learn from this ourselves?

3. This passage shows that God's people can become complacent in defeat, unwilling to trust him and venture out in faith. How might this apply to you?

4. This passage tells us much about 'Judge' Samson, but even more about the Lord, our judge. What new insights about God does this passage give you?

5. What does this passage teach us about spiritual gifts?

6. Trace the progress of sin in the life of Samson. What might you learn from this?

17:1-18:31: Doing the Right Thing?

At first sight the last five chapters of Judges seem rather odd. For a start, neither of the two incidents (chapters 17–18, 19–21) are about the judges! Then, careful observation suggests that both of the incidents, and certainly the second, occurred at the beginning of the period of the judges. Why, then, are they included here?

Most students of the book have concluded from this that chapters 17–21 are an appendix and so, in a sense, they are. However, it is wrong, as some have done, to virtually ignore them. Indeed, it is far more likely that these chapters form a sort of climax to the book (most books work up to a climax at the end!). This is certainly the way in which they will be treated here. Most importantly, they describe the character of the people during this period of Israel's history and illustrate their failure to live before God (chapter 17f.) and man (chapter 19ff.) as they had been called to do.

What was needed (so the refrain implies in 17:6; 18:1; 19:1 and 21:25) was firm, godly, national leadership. At length, of course, even the monarchy failed since not every king was faithful and, more seriously, even a good king could only effect outward obedience to God. What was needed was not only a king 'after the Lord's own heart' but one who was able to undertake an inner transformation of the hearts of his people.

Yet there is a paradox here. It appears that the people did believe they were doing right. As far as they were concerned nothing was wrong. Thus, with a profound dose of irony, the present story is told in such a way that on the surface all seems well. However, it also hints that there is a different perspective to be adopted which, like a good pair of glasses, clears the vision and offers a quite different view!

In many ways these chapters describe a situation so like what we experience today. The Lord was still the object of worship of the Israelites: no other god is mentioned in these two chapters (and note, especially, 17:2, 3, 13; 18:5, 6,10). Yet, in fact, the people, as a whole, had rejected the revelation of God and had constructed what amounted to an entirely new religion under the guise of 'orthodoxy'. It is, perhaps, significant that the name of the Lord is never used by the narrator. It is only ever used on the lips of those whose story is being described!

There is a tragic warning here. And while we can easily point the finger elsewhere we need to see that this danger is one that always stands in the way of evangelicals. Whatever we profess we have to acknowledge: (1) our own ignorance of the Bible, (2) our lack of concern to put the matter right, and (3) our frequent tendency to stand upon rather than sit under the Scripture: a tendency that has led many cults into the grossest error.

The only alternative to revelation is self-invention. It is clear that, first, Micah and his mother, then, the Danites (as well as Jonathan) had imposed their own will and understanding upon what they considered religion ought to be. This was inevitable. Once we have rejected divine revelation there can be no other voice than our own. We believe what suits us! Moreover, once we have turned away from what God clearly says then we are bound to admit that someone else may have insights which we lack. We are willing to consider all religions as on an equal footing. Micah and his mother obviously considered that the Canaanites had something to offer since they were quick to make an idol like theirs (*17:3*).

Again this is a danger to us too. We forget that the Lord is a jealous God and that other gods are non-existent. All too willingly we allow our own ideas and opinions to colour the way we understand true Christianity.

Man-made religion inevitably becomes formal. Proper rites and ceremonies, the manipulation of God for personal gain and a religion devoid of moral demands is the natural result. This was true here. Micah wanted a religion for his own convenience. Significantly, and in comparison with Samson, there is no mention of the Holy Spirit.

We need to look at all of this in a little more detail. The house of God was at Shiloh (*18:31*). But a journey there demanded time and energy. What a splendid idea, then, to have a shrine in the home, **in Micah's house (*17:4*)**! This minimum sort of religion is reflected in Micah's mother. She dedicates **eleven hundred shekels of silver** to the Lord but only used **two hundred shekels** (*17:3,4*) to make a **carved image and a cast idol**; thus holding back all she superstitiously dared!

This selfish attitude lay at the heart of Micah's religion as it so often does in perversions of Christianity. For Micah the purpose of religion is clearly stated in 17:13 when he is reported as saying '**Now I know that the LORD will be good to me**.' He wanted to manipulate God for his own blessing. He wanted to secure cheap grace. And this could be undertaken through the right cultic acts. Thus, he installed both the 'proper' objects of worship (the **image and the idol**, 17:4) and the 'proper' tools of the trade to find out God's will (the **ephod and some idols**, 17:5). The house was full of the trappings of religion, and Micah (whose name means 'Who is like the Lord?') seemed totally unaware that anything was wrong; what he did was right in his own eyes. It was of course an added bonus when a 'real' priest came along (*17:7ff.*) and the 'icing on the cake' must have been the knowledge that he was the grandson of Moses (*18:30*). His shrine was bound to be a winner!

Yet this sort of view of religion is almost inevitably accompanied by gross superstition. This was true in Micah's case. He seemed frightened out of his wits by his mother's curse, not by any sense of wrongdoing (*17:2*). He feared some magical quality in the curse. This same sense of superstition seems to have influenced the Danites and their desire to take the shrine with them to their new territory; after all it had already proved its worth when it had said '**Go in peace. Your journey has the LORD's approval**' (*18:6*). This prediction had proved right since they had been able to find territory and conquer it with ease!

And one of the 'blessings' this sort of religion of cheap grace carries with it is a negligible moral demand. Micah was thoroughly rotten (*17:1, 2*) and he showed no willingness to change. His was a religion without repentance.

At the same time it may be able to claim a successful 'track record'.

Several commentators draw attention to the fact that there are many elements in these two chapters which seem to echo the story of the Exodus. It is difficult to escape the conclusion that this is deliberate. So reflect for a moment! The **Danites** send **warriors ... to spy out the land and explore it** (*18:2*), just as Moses and Joshua had done before. They returned with a good report and, unlike the people of Israel in the past, they encouraged conquest (*18:7-9*). '**Come on, let's attack them**' certainly seems a more faithful response. What is more they were successful; conquest achieved they found a secure homeland at last (*18:27-29*). Small wonder that they were determined to have Micah's shrine and priest join them (*18:14ff.*) and that they found pride of place in their new territory (*18:30f.*).

There are, of course, hints that all is not well. Micah's hopes (*17:13*) soon proved illusory (*18:18-26*). Moreover, for all the fact that the story is one of apparent mighty deeds, we are reminded that the reason that the Danites moved northwards was because **they had not yet come into an inheritance among the tribes of Israel** (*18:1*). Bearing in mind the early chapters of this book (see especially *1:34*), we know that the reason was faithlessness. Moreover, the author of Judges stresses both that the inhabitants of Laish were **peaceful** and had **no-one to rescue them** (*18:27, 28*); they were defenceless. At the same time the Danites acted with extreme brutality (*18:27*) and established their territory outside of the promised land. All is not quite what it might appear and the first interpretation of events may need substantial revision!

If we consider that the grosser forms of religious perversion are more apparent in 'popular' forms of Christianity, we have to beware that the seeds are not found in us. It has to be said that all too easily the balance between grace and obedience is not maintained by us. Moreover, how often we see our religion in essentially selfish terms; we are content with mere formality rather than real service of God. And how often we diminish the biblical emphasis on corporate worship. We can lead an increasingly isolated religion and feel sure that the Lord is for us! First impressions can be false impressions.

Micah's hopes (*17:13*), as we have seen, proved to be a self-delusion (*18:18-26*, especially the last verse). But there was worse. His perversion was adopted by the Danites (*18:27ff.*). This is always the paradoxical and sad truth. False religion will usually spread more readily than the true, even though it is discredited from the start (*17:1f.*). In the end, however, the writer of the Book of Judges knew exactly where all this led (*18:30*): **captivity** (here a reference to the defeat at Aphek and the removal of the Ark, the symbol of the Lord's presence from Israel; see 1 Samuel 4).

The point is clear. The Lord is not manipulated. His blessing is rooted in grace and dependent upon obedient faith. Anything else leads to separation from God.

The saddest thing of all in these two chapters is what it tells us about at least one of the Levites. The Levites had been appointed as the religious leaders and teachers of God's people. They had been given certain villages in which to base their ministries. Jonathan, however, came from Bethlehem which was not one of those villages (*17:7*). Perhaps the reason for this was that Israel's failure to possess the land had meant that the Levites had to find other homes. Perhaps Jonathan himself was at fault. Either way, failure to lead the people spiritually had brought about this sorry state of affairs.

And why was Jonathan looking for somewhere new to live? Had he been rejected or inadequately supported? Or was he a mercenary looking for personal prestige and advancement? In the light of the sequel this is not at all unlikely (*18:19f.*, especially *verse 20*). He was rather like the 'Vicar of Bray' in the old song. He was content to provide the religion the people wanted. He was more interested in profit than being a prophet.

And the great tragedy was that he was a descendant of Moses. As such he seems to have been well-known (*18:3*). From what great heights he had fallen!

How often has it been true that those who ought to have led the Lord's people to him have led in the opposite direction. How important that we are discerning and prayerful for those who lead us. And how important we look for prophets, not merely for those who will pander to our own whims and interests. The last point is one that has been all too often neglected by evangelicals.

There are some important lessons in this passage: lessons which we are inclined to think don't apply to us. But they do! So let us be prayerfully watchful.

Questions:

1. If true religion is founded upon the revelation of God, what sort of place do the Scriptures occupy in your individual and corporate life? What implications for your future conduct arise from your conclusions?

2. What do you expect to get out of your faith? Are your hopes consistent with the teaching of the Bible?

3. False religion, under the guise of orthodoxy, seems to flourish better than the true faith. Why is this sin? How does this passage help us understand such situations?

4. If you are in some form of leadership in the church, what lessons might you learn from the example of Jonathan?

5. Again, reflecting upon the example of Jonathan, what sort of leaders should you be looking for in your church? How might you best support them?

19:1-21:25: Nearly Everything Wrong!

Once again the chorus line of the final chapters of the Book of Judges is heard: **In those days Israel had no king** (*19:1*). In view of what has already happened in the previous two chapters, the words have an ominous ring. Once again we are introduced to a **Levite**; this time, however, one who has no 'aristocratic' family ties and who comes from one of the poorer regions of Israel, the **hill country of Ephraim**.

The story, however, apparently begins well. In ancient Israel, as in many places in the modern world, a marriage involved the payment of a sum of money to the groom's family by the girl's parents. This was understood to provide support to a family group who now had 'an extra mouth to feed'. However, where a family was poor, a girl could be 'sold' as a wife. Thus the family received an income from the girl rather than having to spend beyond its means to find a suitable husband. This process is described in Exodus 21:7-11. The Levite had, apparently, contracted this form of marriage: hence the reference to the girl as a **concubine**. This could be seen as a merciful act by the Levite.

The girl, however, proved **unfaithful** (presumably by committing adultery) and went back home to her father. The Levite resolves after a period of **four months** to persuade her to return to Ephraim. Since the Old Testament law calls for the death penalty for adultery, both the family and the Levite may be regarded as 'out of step' with God's will at this point. However, the same Scriptures emphasise the Lord's mercy and encourage judgment to be tempered with mercy. So, once again, the Levite's action can be seen in the best possible light.

The Levite received a warm welcome and lavish oriental hospitality and the girl seemed content (the reference to her having taken the Levite to her father's house seems a 'coded message' intended to indicate her consent). All seems to be moving towards the scenario 'and they lived happily ever after' (*19:3-8*). Did we correctly hear an ominous note in the words **In those days Israel had no king**?

At length the Levite, unwilling to over-stay his welcome (or, at least, we can read his action this way), resolves to go back home with his wife; even though it is late in the day when the party finally leaves, *19:9,10*). At which point the story does begin to take a turn for the worse; and what a 'worse' it is going to be!

First of all, we are reminded that the city of **Jebus**, or Jerusalem as we know it better, was still in pagan hands; an **alien city** (*19:10-12*). Then we are alerted to the fact that the Levite is fearful about spending a night among (possibly hostile) strangers. So nearby **Gibeah** is chosen. A third worrying note is, however, sounded by the observation that **no-one took them into his home for the night** (*19:15*). Hospitality of strangers was no less expected of the people of God under the Old Covenant as under the New; but here is an entire town turning its back on its God-given responsibility. Two further notes of warning are struck: hospitality is eventually found in the home of another stranger to the town (**an old man from the hill country of Ephraim** (*19:16*) who shows pity on 'one of his own') and who says, '**Only don't spend the night in the square**' (*19:20*). Why?

The slow build-up to the story is brought to a sudden and dramatic climax by the author of the book and in a way that invites comparison with Genesis 19; the story of Sodom and Gomorrah. It is possible that some translations soften the text in verse 22. Certainly, it could be translated 'and the men of the city, sons of Belial'. In other words the city is utterly pagan and its (male) inhabitants, to a man, sodomites. '**Bring out the man ... so that we can have sex with him**,' they cry (*19:22*). But (and this is the shocking thing) these people are **Israelites** (*19:12*)!

Then, just as suddenly, we begin to realise that all that has gone before, has not been all it seemed. The old man offers to sacrifice his **virgin daughter** (*19:24*) and even the Levite's **concubine** to 'save his skin' (though he comes up with a rationale: '**Since this man is my guest, don't do this disgraceful thing**', *19:23*).

When this suggestion seems to be getting nowhere, the Levite acts and sends out his concubine for the crowd to rape and abuse her (*19:25*). But the real shock comes when in the morning he is so callous, '**Get up; let's go**' (*19:28*, a phrase even more abrupt in the Hebrew). No wonder he is called **her master** (*19:27*).

All this gives pause for reflection. What sort of 'wife' was this girl: a housekeeper, a sex-fulfilment object perhaps, whom others can abuse just as the Levite had done. Now, perhaps, we begin to reflect upon the fact that throughout the story the woman has not spoken a word or uttered an opinion (though others have, even the Levite's servant, *19:11*). Under the veneer of 'the compassionate and forgiving man of God' we are alerted to the fact that this man is, himself, corrupt. And if the other religious leaders are like him...!?

The ghoulish sequel – the Levite **took a knife and cut up his concubine, limb by limb, into twelve parts and sent them into all the areas of Israel** – provokes what, at least at first sight, seems an appropriate response: **Everyone who saw it said, 'Such a thing has never been seen or done, not since the day the Israelites came up out of Egypt. Think about it! Consider it! Tell us what to do!'** The Israelites are morally outraged and all of them (an unusual note of unity in this book!) are roused to act (*19:29-30*). But **in those days Israel had no king**. Will their united response show that they stand on higher moral ground?

It is easy to think that a passage such as this has little or nothing to say to us. Granted it has a lot to say to modern society but little or nothing, surely, to the evangelical church. In this, however, we make a great mistake. Nearly every verse of judgement in these three chapters concerns the people of God and their conduct to one another: there is little or no interest in the world outside! The modern analogy puts believers, not the world, under the microscope because they are the New Testament people of God!

Throughout these chapters the concern is with the visible testimony of the community of God's people (see, especially, *19:30*). Certain conduct could be expected (though not approved of) in the world of men but it has no place among the people of God. The Israelites were horrified at the stories of mass homosexuality and rape among themselves. This reflects their conviction that they were called to live the life of God before others, especially in their community life.

We only need to remember Jesus' words in Matthew 5:21ff. to discover how near to home the application of this passage is to us. We can abuse others in the church in other ways than by physical violence. Paul understood this: alongside of the description of acts also described in Judges (sexual immorality, debauchery, drunkenness, orgies etc.) lie sins which, in God's sight are just as bad since they, too, strike at the heart of the witness of the Lord's people (hatred, discord, jealousy, fits of rage, selfish ambition, dissensions). Indeed it is interesting to note that these sins lie at the centre of Paul's list, bracketed by the others (Galatians 5:19-21). Yet how often church life exhibits precisely such attitudes and is content that they remain there. Moreover, too often God's people are oblivious of the fact that not only is the witness of God's people undermined but the intention of the Lord that church life should be heaven on earth is utterly set aside.

Chapter 20, like the previous chapter, appears to begin encouragingly. In response to the report of the horrifying events in Gibeah **all the Israelites from Dan to Beersheba** (a phrase which emphasises *everyone*) turned up. Not only did they turn up but the unity of their response is stressed by the words, **as one man**. Even better, they gathered **before the LORD**, ready for action (*20:1*).

The Levite's story having been repeated (and edited by him to absolve himself from all blame!), the people again as **one man** (*20:8,11*) decide on what appears to be an appropriate response (*20:9ff.*). All *appears* to be well.

Sadly, the Benjamites are unwilling to act against Gibeah and, instead, prepare for civil war (*20:13-15*), with a crack corps of sling throwers (who being left-handed would attack the enemy from a vulnerable angle) ready for action. We begin to fear the consequences even if Benjamin is generally outnumbered.

Nevertheless, the Israelites **went up to Bethel and enquired of God** (*20:18*). A clear answer is given (*verse 18b*) and battle engaged (*verses 19, 20*); but Israel is defeated (*verse 21*)! Just what is going on?

Plans were, however, made for a second battle (*verse 22*) and, grief having been expressed for those lost, Israel again gathered **before the LORD** and **enquired** of him (*verse 23*). Again a clear answer is given. But, once again, Israel is defeated (*verse 25*).

It is at this point that we begin to wonder whether Israel has itself done something wrong! As with so much of this section of Judges we wonder whether things have not been quite what they seem. The sequel suggests that our questions are on track. For Israel returns to Bethel but this time there are several differences. This time **all the people** go up (*20:26*), the grief is deeper and the offering of **burnt offerings and fellowship offerings** suggests that they, themselves, are aware of their own failure. Finally, their question is more hesitant, reflecting a greater desire to know God's will than impose their own (*verse 28*). Perhaps, significantly, **Phinehas** the priest is mentioned as involved on this occasion. (Incidentally, it is this reference to Phinehas, Aaron's grandson, together with the mention of Jonathan, Moses' grandson in chapters 17 and 18, that persuades most scholars to suggest the events of chapters 17-21 occurred early in the period of the Judges.)

All this builds upon the anxiety we, perhaps, felt when we read of the Levite's somewhat gilded description of the events at Gibeah. It makes us pause and reflect that the Israelite response was precipitate. Benjamin was not invited to the tribal gathering (see *20:3*) and the decision taken begins to read rather more like the justice of a lynch-mob. Moreover, when the people first enquired of the Lord it was not to ask what they should do but how they should do it (*20:18*). Israel seemed, however, to have learnt their lesson and God promises '**Go, for tomorrow I will give them into your hands**' (*20:28*).

Battle is enjoined again. New and shrewder tactics are adopted (and described in considerable detail to emphasise what takes place) but, as the author recognises, **the LORD defeated Benjamin** (*20:35*), a defeat which is almost total; a mere **six hundred** men (*20:47*) left as remnant of what was, but a few hours earlier, a tribe of over 26,000 fighting men.

Not all that is described in this chapter is to the credit of Israel, as we have seen above. However, the Israelites were rightly horrified when they realised what was happening among them (*19:30*). They resolved upon action (*20:11*), for behaviour so destructive of community life and witness had to be dealt with (*20:13*); even if they sinfully mishandled it. Not surprisingly they found this led to conflict (*20:13ff.*): it invariably does, for the unspiritual will always side with friends rather than the will of God. Confrontation became both inevitable and, yet, necessary. To the credit of Israel they did not 'duck' or 'fudge' the issue.

Discipline is a word that is unpopular in an indisciplined age. And how quickly we ape the world in its attitudes. How easily, too, we fall into the trap of thinking of the church as a club we have joined (and folk ought to be pleased we have, no matter what) and which we use for our convenience. What a different picture is painted in the Bible! The church is the community of the holy God which he has set apart, and as such all unholiness must be ruthlessly dealt with for his glory.

Of course, in dealing with any failure among the people of God it is so easy to be 'holier than thou'. And we fail, if we act in such a way, to remember that 'there, but for the grace of God, go we'. Moreover, we forget, so often, that it is a brother or sister who has fallen and we lack sorrowful compassion. This was, in part, Israel's sin. Not until they had recognised their own sinfulness and had shed tears over their own shortcomings and that of their brother did they know the Lord's support (see, especially, *20:26-28*).

A further, more negative, lesson that we learn is that the Israelites went into the matter content to depend on their greater strength (compare *20:15,17*). They had to learn the lesson that only utter dependence upon the Lord and a sense of complete weakness would avail. It is a lesson we are sometimes slow to grasp.

Chapter 21 brings both the present story and the Book of Judges to an end – and what a messy end it is! While some might justify Israel's action against Benjamin as just (and argue the tribe which had become 'pagan' should be treated as one of the godless peoples of the land), it seems more likely that, though the Lord gave the victory, the carnage that followed was 'over the top'.

It is easy to try to crack a nut with a sledgehammer when it comes to discipline. Our righteous anger becomes a sinful over-reaction and in the heat of the moment we resolve upon actions which subsequently bring much grief. This seems to have happened to Israel. Thus, calm reflection led to great grief (*21:2f.*) with the people **raising their voices and weeping bitterly**. It also led to an acknowledgement of sin witnessed by the presentation of **burnt offerings and fellowship offerings** (*21:4*).

Again to the credit of the Israelites, they did all they could to put the matter right (*21:6ff.*). We can applaud their wish to heal the breach and admit their mistakes.

Too often we act differently. We consider that to admit a mistake is a sign of weakness, we do not show the attitude of the Lord Jesus who does not quench a smoking flax or break a bruised reed. Discipline is not accompanied by a desire for healing.

Yet there is something bizarre about this chapter. It was at Mizpah that the understandable but foolish oath was made (*21:1*), before the Lord's will had been openly sought by the people. Thus, while they are understandably concerned not to treat their oath lightly (*21:5*), the problem was one which they seemed to have brought upon themselves.

Then we miss any reference to their seeking the Lord's will as they seek to resolve the situation (see *21:6-11*). The result is more carnage; this time Jabesh Gilead is wiped out except for those **four hundred young women who had never slept with a man** (*verse 12*) who are 'culled' as wives for the remaining Benjamite men.

Similarly, when the shortfall of two hundred women is made good by the ruse of the organised kidnapping of some of the young women attending the **annual festival of the LORD in Shiloh** (*21:15-23*), it all seems something of a ruse to escape a technicality. It may be that this dance was a recognised occasion in which spouses were sought and won. Fathers could (by a certain stretch of the imagination) argue that they did not give their daughters but that they were taken, but all this seems special pleading.

What are we intended to make of all this? Technically, as with the incidents described in chapters 17 and 18, the people seem to act according to the letter of the law, yet they also seem to be far from its spirit. Israel may be acting as **one man** (see *20:1* etc.), but, as the final verse of the book reminds us, **everyone did as he saw fit** (*21:25*). Without a godly leadership which sought the Lord, the people all too often resorted to their own devices, even when their motives (as here) seemed good.

We, too, need to be reminded that authority in the church is not found in any of its officers nor in the majority of its members. It is found in King Jesus. He has set before us the way we should live and we are to listen to him. It is to him that we are to look for guidance and help. We ought to want to know what he thinks. When we humbly look to him we shall both individually and collectively begin to live like him — to his glory, our blessing and to the saving of the world (which was Israel's calling, and is ours too)! Failure to do so (even when we try our best) is only likely to lead to the messy special pleading and resolutions that the present chapters describe.

So the book ends without a king, but the Israelites going home to their God-given inheritance (*21:24*). What a testimony to the Lord's grace! How can this muddle-headed people, who only turn to the Lord as a last resort and whose understanding of religion and morality is such as is described in the last five chapters, still be **Israelites** with an **inheritance** in the land to which to return? Sheer grace is the answer. Not, of course, a grace that can be presumed upon (there have been enough warnings about this in the Book of Judges), but grace which can triumph over every disaster that God's people dream up for themselves.

This is the sustained message of the Old Testament. It is the supreme point of the New. Then, God in the person of his Son, enters a sin-soaked world of helpless and hopeless men and women and, in love, sacrifices himself to save them.

Hallelujah. Amazing grace!

Questions:

1. Consider how difficult it sometimes is to distinguish a good motive from a bad one. How can we make such a distinction? Do you examine your motives to determine whether you are really doing the right thing?

2. Faced with a crisis the Levite showed his true colours. How can you and I avoid acting as he did when 'the chips are down'?

3. What lessons are we to learn from this passage about careful examination of issues before we make judgements?

4. We can do the right things for the wrong reasons and in the wrong way. Explore how this is possible in the light of the present passage. Can you think of your own examples?

5. What do we learn from this passage about the importance of doing things God's way? How can we be sure we are in his will?

6. Trace the grace of God through the events of chapters 19–21.

THE BOOK OF RUTH

Introduction

The Book of Ruth has always been a favourite with Bible readers; perhaps because its happy story contrasts with the dark days of the Book of Judges; perhaps because everyone likes a good love story. Whatever the reason and despite some cultural differences (e.g. the gleaning procedure in chapter 2; the marriage proposal of chapter 3; the practice of redemption in chapter 4), the book has a timeless quality which appeals to us all.

Possibly, however, the attractiveness of the book is due to the fact that Ruth is a book about people like us. Ruth was no great leader or heroic sufferer. She was not like a David or a Samuel, a Nehemiah, an Elijah or a Job. She was a simple, ordinary person; just like most of us. Moreover, her experience of God was similar to ours. Hers was not the privilege of a prophet. She did not have great visions. She had no oracles direct from God. Like us, Ruth found God in her daily life. And the same was true of all those around her.

Thus, Ruth is an important book. Most of the stories of the Bible are full of kings and great leaders, of wars and of extraordinary appearances of God. It is sometimes difficult for us to feel the same as such people. But it is not difficult for us to feel like Elimelech and Naomi, Ruth and Orpah, Boaz and the un-named kinsman. How encouraging, moreover, is the fact that the God of the Exodus is also the God of Ruth's move to Bethlehem; the God who provided for a nation in the wilderness is the same God who looked after Ruth and fed her; the God who gave Abraham and Sarah a son is the same God who gave Naomi an heir.

Two commentaries stand out among a number of quite useful works. Robert Hubbard (The Book of Ruth, Eerdmans, 1988) offers up-to-date and detailed comment of the highest order. David Atkinson (The Message of Ruth, IVP, 1983) is biblical exposition at its best; warm and pastorally applied. Excellent.

Other works may be used with profit. For example, Leon Morris (bound with Cundall on Judges, IVP, 1968) gives a good explanation. Among recent studies on Ruth, The Book of Ruth by Murray D. Gow (IVP, 1992) is stimulating; though by no means always followed in this study!

1:1-5: Total Disaster

These verses set the scene for the whole book of Ruth. They are introductory words – but no less significant or important for that. And there are some very practical lessons which remain relevant today.

The words **in the days when the judges ruled** (*verse 1*) hint at how we should understand the early verses of Ruth. They take us back to the Book of Judges where, as we have seen, a repeated cycle of disobedience – disaster–repentance–renewal – is found (especially in the earlier chapters). Probably, the precise time of the Book of Ruth is that of the Midianite conquest described in Judges 6. Judah was, therefore, under the judgment of God for its evil ways (see especially Judges 6:1). This is confirmed by the fact that the land which God had described as 'a land flowing with milk and honey' (Exodus 3:8,17; 13:5; 33:3 etc.) was suffering **famine**. God had threatened famine on the people if they sinned against him (Deuteronomy 28:22-24). Even **Bethlehem**, a place whose name means 'the house of bread', and which was usually a fertile area, was suffering.

How does a people desert God? Only because individuals one by one do so! Therefore we are introduced to one family in Bethlehem. They were probably a wealthy family since we are told that **they went to Moab and lived there** (*verse 2*). Anyone who has moved to a new home knows that it is often an expensive thing to do. Only the richer families in Bethlehem could have afforded to move. Two other references in the text may re-enforce this view. Naomi's comment in verse 21, '**I went out full**' suggests that they had been a wealthy family. In addition to this, the **Ephrathites** (*verse 2*) were descendants of Caleb and may well have been local aristocracy.

The author of the Book of Ruth clearly believed that names could be significant. He introduces us to a man named **Elimelech** – a name meaning 'the Lord is my king'. Perhaps this name expressed the hopes of Elimelech's parents. Possibly it was the name given to him by his contemporaries: a sort of nickname. Sadly, despite his name, Elimelech acted in a thoroughly unspiritual way, as we shall see.

We can sympathise with Elimelech. His two sons are named **Kilion** and **Mahlon**. These were popular names in the ancient Near East but they sounded very like two words meaning 'sickly' and 'pining'. The author of Ruth, who seemed to know a great deal about the family, apparently mentions the names ironically; their names reflected reality. So Elimelech had two sickly sons in a society where sons were essential. Sons would look after their parents when old age came. In time of famine the weak always seemed to suffer first. Doubtless that caused Elimelech great anxiety. Concern for himself and his wife as well as for his sons naturally led him to explore possible ways out of the famine. Eventually he decided to go and live temporarily in Moab.

For an Israelite this was a quite astonishing decision. There are two reasons for this. In the first place, for an Israelite to leave the land which God had given to that nation was equivalent to deserting his God. God's presence was believed to be especially linked to the land. The tent of God (probably at Shiloh) was a symbol and testimony that God was the God of this people in this land. And Elimelech left it!

Secondly, God had made it clear that Moab, a people who worshipped the fire god Chemosh, were a people to be avoided by the people of God (see Deuteronomy 23:3-6 and compare 2 Kings 3:26, 27 and Numbers 21:29). But Elimelech was ready to live with them! He may have rationalised his decision. The Hebrew word underlying **lived there** usually refers to temporary lodgings. However, one year succeeded to another until **ten years** elapsed (*verse 4*).

Moreover, when Elimelech was in Moab he allowed both his sons to marry Moabite women. Deuteronomy 7:3,4 would probably have been understood by the Israelites at the time as including the Moabites and prohibiting marriages between Moabites and Israelites (but see the comment on Ruth 3:1-18). His action may reflect a desire to establish friendly relationships in a community which would have been suspicious of the alien Israelite in their midst and may have made life very difficult for the family and ostracised them. Nevertheless, Elimelech seems to have behaved with hardly a thought for what God required him to do.

In this way, Elimelech is typical of many unspiritual believers. Living in sinful days, he adopted the attitudes of men and women around him and gave little thought to God. He was self-willed and unsubmissive to God. Instead of seeing that the famine was a reason for him to come in repentance to God, he added to his sin; and doubtless he excused his behaviour by appealing to the needs of his family. Here, then, is a son of Jacob acting like a son of Esau, despising his birthright (see Genesis 27). How many Christian 'Elimelechs' do the same today!

Sadly, this passage also describes the consequences of Elimelech's rebellion against God. He had to learn the bitter lesson spelt out in 1 Corinthians 11:27,28; (and note how, unusually, all four Gospels repeat this particular teaching of Jesus: 'For whoever wants to save his life will lose it, but whoever loses his life for me will save it' – Luke 9:24, see Matthew 10:39; Mark 8:35; John 12:25). Thus, the security and protection which Elimelech sought were denied him. Both he (*verse 3*) and, worse still since sons offered security to their parents in old age, his sons (*verse 5*) **died** childless. Thus Naomi **was left without her two sons and her husband** (*verse 5*); a helpless and hopeless woman in a strange land. Indeed, Elimelech's sons, as we have seen, sank to the spiritual level of their father. They entered into disobedient marriages and all came to disaster; selfish rebellion against God (however Elimelech rationalised it) brought disaster on the whole family. Elimelech's sin influenced others to sin and brought disaster on them all.

Questions:

1. 'No man is an island.' Reflect on how this is demonstrated in this passage and draw out the lessons we should learn from this.

2. Note from this passage how easy it is to rationalise away our disobedience to God. How can we avoid falling into the same trap?

1:6-22: The Path of True Discipleship

The remainder of the first chapter of Ruth describes the response of three women – Naomi, Orpah and Ruth – to the challenge of full commitment to God.

Naomi had been an inhabitant of Bethlehem. However, her departure to Moab with her family was, as we have seen, an act of rebellion against God (see *verses 1-5*). She appears to have recognised this when she says, '**The LORD has testified against me**' (*verse 21*). Naomi was like so many of God's children; selfish rebellion had caused her to depart from her God.

But God does not leave his backslidden children alone. He seeks to win them back. Sometimes, as with Naomi, personal disaster is the method he uses. The sorrow of bereavement and loss often awakens a longing for a return to a spiritual walk once more. However, this did not appear to be the case with Naomi. Perhaps her bitterness (see *verse 20*) was too great.

However, eventually her old desires were reawakened when she heard of God's blessing on others back at her home (*verse 6*). She heard of blessing which had followed repentance (see Judges 6:16 for the probable setting) and it was a blessing that offered her hope since the Lord was **providing food for them**. For a widow facing the prospect of hunger in a foreign land, this was enough. So she determined to go home to her people and, it would appear, return to her God.

Naomi had no false hopes of what to expect. She did not expect God's blessing necessarily to follow her. She knew that she might have to live with the consequences of past failure. Later she will say, '**I went away full but the LORD has brought me back empty**' (*verse 21*). Nevertheless it was the Lord who was bringing her back and she would follow him. And when she returned, her life was characterised by joyful trust and obedience to God (see especially *2:20-22*). She had left Israel to secure her family and her food. When she returned it was for these two things especially that she showed humble dependence on God. She had learnt the lesson: 'Trust and obey, for there's no other way to be happy'.

Orpah was the Moabite wife of Kilion (see *4:10*). She must have been a pleasant and lovable young woman. Orpah had stayed with Naomi when she had been widowed rather than return home to her parents. She was clearly fond of her mother-in-law (as *verse 14* demonstrates). She also seemed to share some of the desires of Naomi for her God. We have already seen that Naomi's motive for returning to Israel was a desire to return to God. It is hardly likely that Orpah would have planned to go to Israel except for the same reason (see *verse 6*). So Orpah set out with Naomi and Ruth (*verse 7*).

Naomi's conversation with her daughters-in-law in verses 8-13 has been differently understood by Christian interpreters. However, the most likely explanation of her words is this. Naomi had to face the cost of her own recommitment to the Lord. She was anxious that her daughters-in-law did the same. With great wisdom, therefore, she put the difficulties of commitment to the Lord before them. She did not want them to be deceived as to what they might expect.

If they stayed in Moab they would have the security of a family around them and the prospect of the happiness of a second marriage (*verses 8,9*). The kindness that the two girls had shown to her deserved such a reward.

However, residence in Israel might well mean permanent widowhood (*verses 11-13*) and certainly the loss of old family ties. And why commit themselves to one whose God seemed to have turned against her (*verse 13*).

Sometimes following Jesus has the same consequences for people today. Jesus taught there is a cost to following him (see Mark 8:34-38; 10:42-45). To gain life, we must lose it first. This is not to say, of course, that there is not another side (compare Mark 10:29-31). However, Naomi was pressing on Orpah the cost of discipleship. Sadly, like the rich young ruler (Matthew 19:16-30; Mark 10:17-22; Luke 18:18-30), the demands of discipleship were too great for Orpah. That this is the issue here is seen in Naomi's comment to Ruth: **your sister-in-law is going back to her people and her gods** (*verse 15*).

Christian preachers rarely seem to emphasise the cost of discipleship today. Perhaps they think that they won't get any disciples that way! Naomi, however, was realistic. She knew it was essential to explain the full cost of discipleship to those who might show a desire to be God's children.

In contrast to her sister-in-law, Ruth's resolve was strengthened by Naomi's challenge. If Orpah took the 'sensible' option, Ruth embarked on the adventure of faith. Thus, humbly she pledged her permanent commitment to Naomi, to her people and to her God (*verses 16,17*). Her words show that she had counted the cost and was resolved on a permanent life of discipleship; Naomi was likely to pre-decease her but she had no intention of returning home. So, burning all her bridges behind her, she says, '**Where you die I will die, and there I will be buried.**' Sensibly, when seeing this resolve, Naomi no longer urged Ruth to go back home (*verse 18*).

A number of scholars suggest that, throughout the book of Ruth, there are allusions back to the lives of the patriarchs Abraham, Isaac and Jacob. One such allusion may exist here and a comparison be intended with Abram leaving Ur of the Chaldeans. If this is the case then, as Hubbard helpfully says, 'Ruth's leap of faith outdid Abraham's. She acted with no promise in hand, with no divine blessing pronounced, without spouse, possessions, or supporting retinue. She gave up marriage to a man to devote herself to an old woman – and in a world dominated by men at that!'

In addition to this we need to remember that, while foreigners did sometimes praise Israel's God in Old Testament times (we might recall the Queen of Sheba, Nebuchadnezzar and others), few confessed loyalty to him. What a remarkable woman!

So the two women return to Bethlehem (*verse 19*); Naomi, as the townsfolk recognise, a mere shadow of what she once was and **Ruth the Moabitess** (note the emphasis, *verse 22*), a stranger in a foreign land and potentially hostile environment.

But, and here we detect a glimmer of hope, providentially they arrived as **the barley harvest was beginning** (*verse 22*). Thus they arrived in late April or early May when clear evidence that there would be no general famine that year was already apparent. Moreover, the wheat harvest would follow about a fortnight later (compare *2:23*). As with so much that is described in the Book of Ruth, there are hints here that the Lord is orchestrating events from the wings! So, we are led to wonder, will Naomi be full again? Will Ruth find home and family among the people of God? And will she, having sacrificed more than Abraham, find a significant place within the history of the people of God? Just what will the Lord do with these two women?

Questions:

1. Reflect upon the ways that the Lord brought Naomi back to himself and Ruth to faith. What does this teach us about the way he leads us to himself?

2. Trace the providential hand of God through this story. What encouragement should we derive from this?

3. What can we learn from this passage about the costs and the blessings of discipleship?

4. Reflect on Naomi's words in verse 21. Was she right to say what she did? Justify your answer!

2:1-23: As Luck Would Have It!

The stories of the Bible are usually told without comment by their authors. No morals are draw from the stories. Sensitive readers are left to work out for themselves the lessons built into the stories. This is true of the Book of Ruth. It is especially true of this chapter. The story is a simple one. Ruth, in trying to secure enough food for herself and Naomi, finds a rich patron in Boaz (a man who, the author hints, may become more than patron!). However, lying behind these events are several great truths.

The first great lesson is this: when people become disciples of the Lord it changes their way of life. Boaz recognised that God had become, for Ruth, one **under whose wings you have come to take refuge** (*verse 12*). As an Israelite, he had done the same and his cry '**The Lord be with you**' (*verse 4*) appears to be more than mere formality. The result in both of them was a life of delighted obedience to God. This is a mark of spiritual maturity: though here it is shown even in a young 'convert' like Ruth.

This truth is most clearly seen in Boaz. In the Old Testament law God had demanded that at harvest time the harvester was not to reap right into the corners of his fields. He was also told not to pick up what was left after the reapers had gone, nor to go back to collect a forgotten sheaf. We read about this in Leviticus 19:9; 23:22 and Deuteronomy 24:19. The reason for these commands was that God wanted his people to show a concern for the poor and needy. He wanted them to show compassion to people like Ruth and Naomi.

The unscrupulous man could, of course, easily neglect this duty. This is suggested in the present passage. Ruth recognised that to exercise the right very much depended on finding **favour** (*verse 2*). And even where gleaning was allowed there might be the discouragement of being **harmed** (*verse 22*); a farmer might be unwilling to protect someone who was in his field on sufferance! Alternatively, such a man could find ways around God's laws (as the Books of Judges and Ruth have already demonstrated on many occasions). However, when we read about Boaz, he not only obeys the letter of the law but he also fulfils its intention. Thus he accedes to Ruth's polite ('**please**') and somewhat bold request (**to gather among the sheaves**, *verse 7*). But, in addition, he offers protection (*verse 15*), assists her productivity by allowing her to drink from water that others drew (thus saving her the effort, *verse 9*), provides her with enough lunch for both her and Naomi (*verses 14,18*), and ensures that she has sufficient from which to glean (*verses 15,16*). All this enables Ruth to return with a **ephah** of grain (*verse 17*), about 15 kilos weight and equivalent to half a month's normal wage at the time!

We can understand the author's response to this: 'As luck would have it' (*verse 3*, so Hubbard). However, the text hints that there is more than random luck at work here. Once again, hidden in the wings, the Lord is at work.

So, in his dealings with Ruth, Boaz is seen as considerate, tender, compassionate, generous and kind. It was that kind of attitude that God's law was intended to promote. Ruth recognised the significance of this action of Boaz. Thus, in verse 10 she asked: '**Why have I found such favour?**' The word 'favour' is one of the most important words in the Old Testament. It is the word which describes the unmerited mercy which God shows to his children. It also describes the response of God's children to him, to one another and then to all. Ruth recognised Boaz's God-like character and, in that way, recognised him as a true disciple of the Lord.

Boaz, of course, recognised the same in Ruth. Though she is a **foreigner** by race (*verse 10*), she has converted to the religion of Israel and, as such, deserves his blessing because she has demonstrated her faith in what she had done for Naomi (*verse 11*). The Bible never tires of teaching this lesson. A true disciple is a person who has met God. That meeting must change a person's life. The disciple's life will now be a copy (imperfect, of course) of God's life and character. Delighted love for God will be the result; a love delighting in all God's wishes and fulfilling the intention of all his words.

Above all, in the New Testament we are shown Jesus as our example. Jesus who 'in very nature God, did not consider equality with God something to be grasped, but made himself nothing, taking the very nature of a servant, being made in human likeness. And being found in appearance as a man, he humbled himself and became obedient to death – even death on a cross! Therefore God exalted him to the highest place and gave him the name that is above every name, that at the name of Jesus every knee should bow, in heaven and on earth, and under the earth, and every tongue confess that Jesus Christ is Lord, to the glory of God the Father' (Philippians 2:5-11). These well-known words follow Paul's admonition: 'Your attitude should be the same as that of Christ Jesus.' We are expected to be copies of Jesus himself! How rarely this lesson is learnt.

Sometimes it is suggested that a spiritual life will be harsh and unattractive. We sometimes meet such supposedly godly people. However, a truly spiritual life is lovely and attractive. We can see this to be true in this chapter. Ruth and Boaz shine forth as attractive and really human people. It is this very fact that draws us to this chapter and makes us delight in the story. But it is also a lesson that all disciples need to learn. True believers are to be attractive because the favour of God to them makes them attractive.

There is no part of life that is uninfluenced by discipleship. This is clearly shown in this chapter. Discipleship is seen in the home. Ruth showed a tenderness and a respect for her ageing mother-in-law (*verse 2*). Naomi had no right to expect all that Ruth did for her. But, then, Ruth was a true disciple. A true disciple does not think about rights, but about needs and responsibilities. Because God had been merciful to Ruth in her needs, she now shows the same attitude to Naomi. In the Bible there is teaching which emphasises that discipleship will be seen in the home. Look up especially Ephesians 5:1, 2, 22-6:4.

Discipleship is also to be seen in the work-place. Ruth's conduct was respectful. She said '**please**' in verse 7, even when taking her rights! Her hard work was immediately noticed (*verse 7b*). Similarly Boaz the rich landowner was generous (*verse 1*); he sought to help the needy; he was approachable, friendly and compassionate (*verses 4,5*). He used his God-given privileges to serve God. We are to do the same. (Compare Ephesians 6:5-9.)

We ought also to notice that when God's mercy has been experienced, a person's attitudes are changed. We have already seen this but it needs emphasising. Ruth was willing to take the most menial and degrading part (*verse 2*). Service for God in the service of others led her to set aside her dignity. Yet how often do we proudly defend ours.

In addition, we see how mercy had led to childlike dependence on God. This is seen in Boaz (*verse 4*) and Naomi, who was so quick to notice God's provision for her (*verses 19,20*). Above all, we see this truth in Ruth's wide-eyed wonder at God's provision for her in the most ordinary of circumstances (*verse 10*). The result of such an attitude is seen in these verses. There is a peace and tranquillity both in need and in plenty. May we show the same spirit!

Another great lesson to learn from this chapter is the faithful care of God for his children, even in hard times. This is especially seen in Ruth's experience. Perhaps it is helpful at this point to remind ourselves what Ruth's needs were:

i) She had the obvious needs that a widow would have. In the ancient world, a widow without a family was a most pathetic person. Often such people were very poor. They depended on the charity of others. Many were forced to turn to prostitution since their bodies were the only resources that they could sell.

ii) Ruth was an alien. She was friendless in a foreign land. This fact is repeatedly emphasised in 2:2,6,10,11,21. Many immigrants to a new country will understand how Ruth must have felt.

iii) She had been recently bereaved and must therefore

have been under great emotional strain. Boaz seems to recognise this in verse 11.

iv) She was a recent convert. Days later, the great confession of 1:16-17 was now being put to the test in the severest way possible.

These things must have filled Ruth with doubts and fears. Some believers today try to hide behind empty spiritual words and are not always honest about their problems. However, most of us if we are honest have experienced at some time the same sort of difficulties as Ruth did. This is one of the reasons why the Book of Ruth is so useful to us. Let us notice, then, how God met Ruth's needs.

Firstly, Ruth began to meet her own needs! Common sense (often lacking in God's people), led to careful thought and sensible action (*verses 2, 3 and 7*) and proved to be part of God's guidance for her. She did what she could and left what she couldn't do in the hands of God.

Secondly, Ruth sought the advice of others close to her (*verse 2*) and found the will of the Lord in their sensible advice. Indeed she discovered God's care for her on a number of occasions in the same way. She found God's care in the tenderness, compassion and generosity of others (*verses 8,9*). That was another way in which God provided for her.

Thirdly, Ruth found (as we have seen) God directly at work in her circumstances. Humanly, by complete coincidence, God led her steps to Boaz, the person most able to help her! This fact was noticed by the author of Ruth (*verse 3*).

All this leads to some very practical lessons. We notice that God's provision was not miraculous. Many believers have an exaggerated regard for miracles. They do not seem to think that God is at work if they have not experienced a miracle. For them, the Book of Ruth may be disappointing. There is no hint of a miracle here. But God does provide for her and for those of us (i.e. for most believers) whose lives are as free of miracle as Ruth's. This is a great comfort. If God provided for her in her ordinary, unexciting, day-to-day experience, he can and will do the same for us!

Moreover, God is seen to be at work in all Ruth's affairs – and in her case they were mostly small ones! What comfort this is to us in our 'small' lives!

It is also important to notice that there is no dramatic change in Ruth's life (not yet, at least!). Rather God showed himself in his daily, detailed attention to her in the middle of all her needs. God did not suddenly deliver her. He met her where she was.

It is this fact which enabled her, and should enable us, to trust him even in the middle of our needs. Boaz's wish – **May the Lord repay you for what you have done. May you be richly rewarded by the Lord, the God of Israel, under whose wings you have come to take refuge** (*verse 12*) – should become a conviction which, by faith, governs our lives as it did Ruth's.

But there is one further thread that runs through this chapter. Ruth and Naomi had returned to Bethlehem facing the prospect of famine, being without family and with the family 'name' in danger of obliteration if no child is born to Naomi (not to mention that young Ruth has no husband!). However, in this chapter the first need has already been met (at least for the time being). Might the Lord make good the other needs too? As the story has unfolded the author has offered hints as to what might yet be. Boaz is from **the clan of Elimelech** and he is wealthy (*verse 1*); his prayer in verse 12 encourages us to look for an answer to Ruth's needs; and Naomi's excitement and reference to Boaz being **one of our kinsman-redeemers** (*verse 20*) all leave the reader with a sense of anticipation mitigated only by the comment in verse 23 – **So Ruth stayed close to the servant girls of Boaz to glean until the barley and wheat harvests were finished. And she lived with her mother-in-law.** – that contact between Ruth and Boaz seems (temporarily?) ended.

Questions:

1. What does this passage teach us about God's demands upon our home life and our social contact with people? In what areas of conduct might you need to rethink and act differently in the light of this passage?

2. Ruth and Boaz thought of responsibilities rather than rights. How might their attitude change your approach to life?

3. Ruth and Naomi were quick to count their blessings and see the hand of God in the smallest details of life. What lesson might you draw from their example?

3:1-18: Home for the Homeless?

The story of Ruth 3 is fairly clear; Naomi takes steps to find Ruth a suitable husband. Several observations need, however, to be made to explain some of the details of the story.

First, to the modern reader (especially in the western world) there do seem to be things done here which we might think wrong. It seems likely that some custom unknown to us, but acceptable at that time, is described here. We need to avoid being critical of the conduct of Naomi, Ruth and Boaz in this chapter. The author of Ruth does not judge them; nor should we. On the other hand, we should not copy them, either!

There is no suggestion that anything immoral took place between Boaz and Ruth; indeed the narrator of the story seems to deliberately choose a word for **lie here** (*verse 13*) which excludes the idea of any sexual indiscretion. Indeed, Boaz probably sent Ruth away early in the morning in order to avoid any possibility of gossip about their conduct which might have hindered his plans for Ruth. Equally, he probably did not send her away in the night where she might be mistaken for a prostitute and vulnerable to attack.

And the verses do not tell us that Boaz was drunk. He was in good spirits. The harvest was good and he had enjoyed a good meal. The Bible does not criticize people for being happy. But it does warn of the dangers of drinking too much alcohol and of the sin of drunkenness.

Secondly, there are two Old Testament practices which are strange to us but are mentioned in this chapter.

The first is *the levirate*. To understand this it is good to look up Genesis 38 and especially Deuteronomy 25:5-10. In Old Testament times it was vital that a man's family name was preserved. Accordingly, if he died without an heir, steps were to be taken to ensure that he had an heir who could carry his name (and inherit his property). Thus it was customary, and required by God's law, that the widow of a dead man be married to one of her husband's relatives. The first son of such a marriage would then be the dead man's heir.

Elimelech had died heirless; or at least his sons died soon after his death, without having had any children themselves. Now only Ruth held out any possibility that Elimelech might have heirs. But Ruth was only his daughter-in-law and no duty rested on her to raise children to keep alive Elimelech's name. Boaz recognised the generosity of Ruth toward Elimelech's family when, in verse 10, he says, '**This kindness is greater than that which she showed earlier**'. Ruth's commitment to Naomi, the responsibility she had assumed for her well-being etc., was a remarkable example of sacrificial kindness. But now Ruth was willing to forego the possibility of a marriage for money or love (*verse 10*) by appealing to Boaz as the kinsman-redeemer (*verse 9*); something even Naomi had not asked of her (compare Naomi's suggestion at the beginning of the chapter to Ruth's proposal in verse 9).

What, then, was the *kinsman-redeemer* (this translates a Hebrew word 'Goel' meaning 'to recover or redeem')? This person is mentioned in Leviticus 25:25-28, 47-49; verses which describe the responsibility of a near kinsman to do all that was necessary to secure the land and support the persons of poor near-of-kin. As we shall see,

Naomi had such a kinsman (chapter 4) who had showed no great desire to fulfil his obligations. Boaz, by contrast, was under no immediate obligation to Naomi but was willing to help her.

We need to ask the question at this point; was Boaz right to want to marry Ruth? In chapter 1 we suggested that Mahlon was wrong to marry Ruth because she was a Moabite. How then could it be right for Boaz to marry her? The answer is this. Although the Old Testament laws seem to be racist, this was never in fact the case. Whoever identified with the people of God was given the full status of an Israelite. The prohibitions against marriage with someone from another race were intended to teach that God hated his people to marry outside the people of God. The Old Testament laws were not so much racist as religious. The people of God were to marry only others from among the people of God and that is the point that is important here. In chapter 1 Mahlon married a worshipper of Chemosh. That was quite wrong. However, after Ruth's confession in 1:16,17 her words and her actions have shown that she was a true worshipper of God. No obstacle, therefore, existed any longer for an Israelite to marry her. Indeed both Ruth and Boaz show such a spiritual maturity in chapter 2 that Boaz could clearly have done no better than marry Ruth! The way that the author of Ruth repeatedly commends her credentials is intended to stress this point.

With these facts in mind we can observe several important lessons which are contained in chapter 3.

In these verses we have a wonderful illustration of the commitment of both Ruth and Boaz to their Lord. It is probable that Mahlon died shortly after marrying Ruth. Otherwise they would probably have had some children, since family planning was largely unknown in the ancient world. Marriage usually occurred soon after puberty and it is probable that no great time elapsed between the death of Ruth's husband and her migration to Israel (the ten years of 1:4 probably refers to the family's stay in Moab rather than the length of the marriages). Ruth was, therefore, probably only in her middle or late teens when the events described in this chapter took place. Possibly she was between the ages of 15 and 18. Boaz was obviously an older man (*verse 10*), probably at least twice her age. However, despite the fact that Ruth was clearly marriageable and could most probably have found a more 'suitable' husband, she chose Boaz. Showing remarkable spiritual maturity for one of her age and experience, Ruth recognised that faithfulness to the intention of God's Word required her to marry a kinsman of Elimelech. In his response to Ruth (*verses 10-13*) Boaz showed he recognised Ruth's obedience to God. He himself (see especially chapter 4) then showed the same obedience to the intention of God's Word.

For both Ruth and Boaz these were costly decisions to make. But they were both motivated by a desire to obey God in all things. In obedience, as we shall see, they found joy and blessing. The same obedience is required of us.

Once again we notice that Ruth and Boaz fulfil God's Word by meeting its deepest concerns. Strictly speaking, Ruth had no obligation to Elimelech. Similarly, Boaz did not have a obligation to Elimelech either. But they both knew that God's laws were intended to show his deep concerns for the welfare of his people. Thus they both went beyond mere obedience to the letter of the law, to the fulfilling of its intention.

Such obedience is expected of every true disciple. Jesus said: 'A new commandment I give to you that you love one another as I have loved you' (John 13:34,35). Though they did not have the full light of the gospel, we can see that Ruth and Boaz were obedient to God in precisely this way. How much more we, who also have the example of Jesus to follow, should follow their example.

One final lesson emerges from this chapter. In the New Testament, Jesus is revealed as the great 'kinsman-redeemer'. In a real sense, Boaz by his actions foreshadowed Jesus. Consider the following facts:

i) A 'goel' had to be a kinsman. Jesus became like us, to be our kinsman-redeemer (see Hebrews 2:17,18).

ii) Jesus loved God and delighted to do God's will. So did Boaz.

iii) Boaz's redemption of Ruth was expensive (see chapter 4). Jesus gave up his own life to pay the price of our redemption.

iv) By redeeming Ruth, Boaz made her his wife. In so doing, he was ready to share his bed with a penniless alien. By redeeming us, Jesus has made us his bride and has been ready to share himself with his enemies.

v) Boaz acted to provide a future for hopeless Ruth. How much more has Jesus done in securing our eternal glory.

Again the chapter ends with us on tip-toe. With another **six measures of barley** the threat of famine recedes still further (*verses 15, 17*). The possibility now exists that Ruth may find a husband and Naomi an heir. But the 'Lord in the wings' still has much to do! There is the kinsman-redeemer nearer than Boaz (*verse 12*) and even if marriage is consummated, will a child be born to a woman who had no children by her previous marriage, and will it be the male child needed to continue Elimelech's line?

Questions:

1. Everything about this story seems to assume that the Lord is in the wings 'orchestrating' what takes place. Yet Naomi, Ruth and Boaz all go about their life planning, even scheming for the result they desire. Reflect upon what this teaches us about our responsibility and God's sovereign ordering of our lives.

2. Consider the sacrifices that Ruth made and which are reflected in this chapter. Are there areas of your own life where similar challenges are placed before you? How should you respond?

4:1-17a: Future Secured

With these verses the Book of Ruth reaches its climax. Once again, the sensitive reader is expected to discern for himself the lessons which lie in the story.

Boaz is as good as his word and, according to ancient oriental custom, waited at the **town gate** (*verse 1*) where, in the wide market place, the town's public business was usually undertaken. When the **kinsman-redeemer** arrives he is invited to a discussion before a number of senior members (**elders**) of the community deemed able to complete the matter.

The mention of **the piece of land that belonged to our brother Elimelech** (*verse 3*) is a new and surprising turn. It suggests that Boaz has given the matter some thought and worked out the most likely way to achieve his purpose.

However, at first the affair takes an apparent turn for the worst! Emphatically, the kinsman-redeemer says, '**I will buy it**' (*verse 4*). Reflection indicates that this was highly predictable. Since it is unlikely that Naomi will have a child, purchase of the land would increase the kinsman-redeemer's real estate. Few able to do so would have passed up the opportunity now being offered!

At this point Boaz plays his 'trump card'. With the land comes Ruth **in order to maintain the name of the dead with his property** (*verse 5*). This is a far less attractive proposition since the man would be required to marry Ruth (**acquire the dead man's widow** conveys this thought) and the income derived from the land would not go directly to the redeemer's estate. Moreover, his own estate would possibly have to be divided with Ruth's children. With an expectant intake of breath we await the reply!

'**I cannot redeem it**' (*verse 6*) elicits in us a silent, 'Hurrah'; Ruth has a home!

But there are still some issues to be resolved. How will they turn out? Frustratingly the author of Ruth slows up the story, probably in order to arouse our interest for the great climax of the story which he has prepared us for with such skill. Whoever thought land conveyancing exciting (*verses 7-10*)?

The sense of movement to a climax is also heightened by verses 11 and 12. **Rachel and Leah** were the founding mothers of Israel. **Perez**, also born of a foreigner, became a famous clan-chief in the nation. What may we expect from the marriage of this remarkable stranger who has dominated the present story?

First of all, however, the marriage needs to take place, a conception occur and a son be born! Just so, says the narrator (*verse 13*); emphasising at this point that the LORD in the wings **enabled her to conceive**.

Secondly, since the story has been preoccupied with the provision of a 'son' for Naomi, we are introduced to the fact that **Obed** (as he was named, *verse 17*), was, apparently, brought up by Naomi as though he were her own child (*verse 16*).

But now, wait for it: **Obed...was the father of Jesse, the father of David** (*verse 17b*)! Whatever we might have expected this surpasses everything; David's great granny is Ruth! And just in case we missed it the first time, a fuller genealogy is offered (*4:18-22*, see below). What a triumph of God's providence and grace!

Before drawing this book to a close, however, there are several remarkable features in this chapter which should not be missed. In particular there are some striking contrasts. First, there is a contrast between Boaz and the other, un-named, kinsman-redeemer. The nameless man was only willing to act on behalf of Naomi and Ruth if it were to his advantage. This, as we have seen, decided the matter for him (*verse 6*). Doubtless the same sort of obstacles lay in Boaz's way as well. However, Boaz was ready to follow the path of obedience to God whatever the consequences.

Too often we only do what is right because it suits us. We need to learn from Boaz. Once again we notice that Boaz was motivated by mercy (see *2:13*) as one who had received mercy.

At this point, however, the author of Ruth plays a subtle joke on his readers. He must have known the name of the kinsman. After all, he knew a great deal about Elimelech and his relatives. However, he does not reveal the name and surely he does not do so quite deliberately! The un-named kinsman acted to secure his name: but it has long since been lost. Boaz 'risked' the loss of his name; and he is not only named but his fame will live on till the end of the world!

As we saw earlier, Jesus taught the same truth (see Matthew 10:39; Mark 8:35; Luke 9:24; John 12:25). It is the great message of the Book of Ruth; to hold fast to our own ambitions will lead to the loss of all. Faithful obedience to God will enable us to inherit eternal life, a lasting inheritance and an honourable name before God.

This same point is made by another contrast in this chapter. In chapter 1 Naomi was described as bereaved and hopeless (*1:5,12,20*). In chapter 4 she has comfort in her old age made sure by the birth of a grandson (*4:13-17*). In her own experience, Naomi had to learn the lesson of obedience. She also learnt that God is merciful to the person who turns his children back from a path of folly. Finally, of course, she learned that God was far more merciful to her than she deserved.

The final contrast in this section is seen in Ruth herself. In chapter 1 she was a friendless, penniless and childless stranger. However, she put her faith in the God of Israel (*1:17,18*). In chapter 4 the same Ruth has not only become the object of a levir's attentions (see chapter 3) but is his wife (*verses 10,13*)! She is the centre of an admiring community (*verse 15*) and the mother of a son (*verse 13*). To have a son was a blessing indeed in the ancient world. Thus Ruth found that her sacrifice was rewarded by God. God is never anyone's debtor. As we follow him, we will learn the same lessons.

Questions:

1. List the undeserved blessings that the Lord gave to Naomi, Ruth and Boaz in this chapter. Then draw up your own list of similar blessings. Finally, reflect upon the mercies of God to you.

2. At first it appeared that Ruth and Boaz's plan was not going to work out. What can you learn from the fact that it did work out and did so in a way they could never have imagined?

4:17b-22: Grace Upon Grace

In this list of names we have a lovely postscript to the book of Ruth. In 1:1 our thoughts were directed back to the Book of Judges. In that book there is one phrase that is regularly repeated. In Judges 17:6; 18:1; 19:1; 21:25 we are told that 'there was no king in those days'. This is not a careless or accidental repetition. In Old Testament times the life of the nation was seen as closely linked to the life of the king. His example set the example which his people were expected to follow. But in the time of the Judges there was no such example. Everyone did 'as he saw fit' (Judges 21:25). The people were, then, in need of a leader after God's own heart. This is the verdict of the Book of Judges. The Book of Ruth picks this thought up. It tells us of a farmer in Bethlehem and a stranger from Moab who lived not for themselves but for God. It shows that their faithfulness was part of God's plan to meet the needs of all his people and to bless them more abundantly than they could ever have imagined. Ruth bore a son who was to be the grandfather of Israel's greatest king, David. And David himself was a king among whose descendants 'great David's greater Son' would be born.

David Atkinson concludes his study on Ruth with these words: 'his life (that is, Jesus) in terms of physical descent was linked to the story of a Moabite girl gleaning in a barley field miles from home; to a caring mother-in-law and a loving kinsman; to a night-time conversation at the threshing-floor; to the willingness of a wealthy farmer to go beyond the requirements of the law in his care for the needy. In short, it is in the ordinariness of the lives of ordinary people that God is working his purposes out. Future significant lives were bound up with the history of Ruth.'[1]

Doubtless those very qualities which David possessed were the fruit of a great-grandparental example (how of-

1. Atkinson, p. 126.

ten is this true!). Thus Ruth and Boaz's apparently insignificant lives are seen to be of vital importance for us all. What an encouragement to our own faithfulness and obedience, even though we may feel ourselves to be insignificant.

Finally, the Book of Judges ended emphasising the amazing grace of God. The Book of Ruth does the same. For this story began with two women; one in rebellion against God, the other a pagan worshipper of Chemosh, the god of Moab. As the story has unfolded we have come to anticipate the Lord's blessing on these two women and our expectations have not been dashed. But all has been of grace.

Questions:

1. What evidence do you have in your life of the amazing grace of God?

2. What encouragement is there in this passage to faithful service of God in 'our small corner'?

3. Can you think of anyone you know whose quiet and faithful witness has brought unexpected blessing? What might you learn from this?

Spiritual Lessons from Judges

The Book of Judges highlights the following lessons.

God:
1. He is a holy and righteous God and hates sin and half-hearted faith.
2. His grace and mercy triumph over human sinfulness and failing.
3. His ability far outstrips human resources.
4. He works in the real 'messy' world.
5. He moves in 'mysterious ways his wonders to perform'.
6. He shows great tenderness in dealing with his people.

True religion:
1. Is a religion of revelation.
2. Knowing God and trusting obedience in his promises is the way to victory, to growth and to the assurance of his 'ever present' help.
3. True religion is a religion for the whole of life.
4. True religion is not to be 'consumer driven'.
5. There are none too old, too inexperienced, too handicapped, too marginalised, too timid that God cannot accomplish (through such weaknesses) his glorious purposes.

Snares that lie before the believer:
1. Presumption upon gifts and graces is dangerous.
2. Compromise brings catastrophe.
3. There is real danger of becoming 'comfortable' in defeat.
4. Persistent sin leads to a downward moral and spiritual spiral and ultimately self-destructs.

Warnings for the community of faith

1. Jealousy and division within the people of God and the failure to see where God is at work leads to disaster.
2. Power corrupts ... Leaders beware!
3. People seldom reach higher standards than those shown by their leaders.

The Book of Ruth

Among the most important lessons to be learnt from the Book of Ruth are the following:

God

1. Sometimes works 'in the wings'; unseen by his children.
2. God works in all things (providence) just as much as he did when he created the world.
3. His gospel is a message for all nations.
4. He is no one's debtor.

True Spirituality

1. Is seen in a life wholly lived according to the revealed will of God.
2. Requires that the cost of following the LORD is counted.
3. Demands a radical change of lifestyle.
4. Is a beautiful thing: it lives beyond the mere letter of the law.
5. Is seen in the service of others.
6. Is not passive but in humble dependence on God 'works out its own salvation'.

A final warning:

Those who seek to save their lives will lose them.